D1169388

Connections: Key Themes in World History

THE FIRST HORSEMAN

Disease in Human History

John Aberth

PEARSON

Prentice
Hall

Upper Saddle River, New Jersey 07458

Library of Congress Cataloging-in-Publication Data

Aberth, John, (date)
    The first horseman : disease in human history / John Aberth.
        p. cm.
    Includes bibliographical references and index.
    ISBN 0-13-189341-6
    1. Communicable diseases—History.   2. Plague—History.   3. Smallpox—History.   4. AIDS
(Disease)—History.
    [DNLM: 1. Communicable Diseases—history.   2. Disease Outbreaks—history.   3. Acquired
Immunodeficiency Syndrome—history.   4. Communicable Disease Control.   5. Plague—history.
6. Smallpox—history.   WA 11.1 A147f 2007]   I. Title.

    RA643.A24 2007
    616.9'09—dc22

                                                                                    2006003601

Editorial Director: Charlyce Jones Owen
Executive Editor: Charles Cavaliere
Editorial Assistant: Maria Guarascio
Marketing Manager: Emily Cleary
Marketing Assistant: Jennifer Lang
Production Liaison: Marianne
    Peters-Riordan
Manufacturing Buyer: Ben Smith
Art Director: Jayne Conte
Cover Design: Kiwi Design
Cover Illustration/Photo: Courtesy
    of the Conway Library, Courtauld
    Institute of Art, London

Director, Image Resource Center:
    Melinda Reo
Manager, Rights and Permissions:
    Zina Arabia
Manager, Visual Research: Beth Brenzel
Manager, Cover Visual Research &
    Permissions: Karen Sanatar
Image Permission Coordinator:
    Cynthia Vincenti
Composition/Full-Service Project
    Management: Chella Sundaram / Integra
    Software Services

Credits and acknowledgments borrowed from other sources and reproduced, with permission, in this textbook appear on appropriate page within text.

Copyright © 2007 by Pearson Education, Inc., Upper Saddle River, New Jersey 07458.
Pearson Prentice Hall. All rights reserved. Printed in the United States of America. This publication is protected by Copyright and permission should be obtained from the publisher prior to any prohibited reproduction, storage in a retrieval system, or transmission in any form or by any means, electronic, mechanical, photocopying, recording, or likewise. For information regarding permission(s), write to: Rights and Permissions, Department.

Pearson Prentice Hall™ is a trademark of Pearson Education, Inc.
Pearson® is a registered trademark of Pearson plc
Prentice Hall® is a registered trademark of Pearson Education, Inc.

Pearson Education LTD.
Pearson Education Singapore, Pte. Ltd
Pearson Education, Canada, Ltd
Pearson Education–Japan
Pearson Education Australia PTY, Limited

Pearson Education North Asia Ltd
Pearson Educación de Mexico, S.A. de C.V.
Pearson Education Malaysia, Pte. Ltd
Pearson Education, Upper Saddle River,
    New Jersey

ISBN 0-13-189341-6

Contents

reword

Connections: Key Themes in World History focuses on specific issues of world historical significance from antiquity to the present by employing a combination of explanatory narrative, primary sources, questions relating to those sources, a summary analysis ("Making Connections"), and further points to ponder, all of which combine to enable readers to discover some of the most important driving forces in world history.

The increasingly rapid pace and specialization of historical inquiry has created an ever-widening gap between professional publications and general surveys, especially surveys of world history. The purpose of *Connections* is to bridge that gap by placing the latest research and debates on selected topics of global historical significance, as well as some of the evidence upon which historians base their insights, into a form and context that is comprehensible to students and general readers alike.

Two pedagogical principles infuse this series. First, students master world history most easily if allowed to focus on specific themes and issues. Such themes, by their very specificity, as well as because of their general application, enable students to perceive and understand the overall patterns and meaning of our shared global past more clearly than is possible through reading, by itself, a massive world history textbook. Second, students learn best when asked to think critically about what they are studying. So far as the study of history is concerned, critical thinking necessarily involves analysis of primary sources.

To that end, we offer a series of brief, tightly focused books that embrace a radical simplicity and a provocative format. Each book goes to the heart of a key theme, phenomenon, or issue in world history – something that has connected humans across cultures, continents, and time spans. By actively engaging with this material, the reader comes to understand in a nuanced and meaningful manner how often distantly located human cultures have been connected to one another as key actors in the epic story of world history.

Alfred J. Andrea
Series Editor
Professor Emeritus of History
University of Vermont

Series Editor's Preface

In 1976 William H. McNeill published *Plagues and Peoples*. With characteristic boldness, McNeill sketched the history of the relationship between *microparasites* (bacteria, viruses, protozoa, and similar microbes that invade and alter the cells of living beings) and *macroparasites*, the greatest and most parasitical of whom are humans and the societies that they create. Admittedly raising more questions than offering definitive answers, McNeill argued that with the rise of "civilized diseases," namely diseases that became endemic in settled communities, these two sets of parasites – the microscopically small and the far-larger, bipedal variety – established a symbiosis that has lasted for at least the last 10,000 years. Simply put, whereas pathogens need hosts in order to replicate and survive, humans have related to the germs that invade their bodies in a variety of ways as they have extended their domination over and exploitation of the world. Strange as it sounds, disease has often served human communities, usually with those communities not fully aware of the nature of their ally. Some of the more obvious examples of this alliance are diseases that aid a community or state in extending dominion over its rivals and infectious agents that act as a defense against invaders who lack adequate defenses against them. Just as often, perhaps more so, disease has come like a thief to rob human communities, small and great, of their vigor and populations, thereby precipitating their collapse and even disappearance. Or, when it did not totally destroy a society, the onslaught of disease in its epidemic form has often precipitated cultural adaptation and even radical alteration of a society's ways of life and even modes of belief.

In the 30 years since publication of McNeill's book, other historians have refined and expanded upon his insights. Thus, O.A. Bushnell's *The Gifts of Civilization: Germs and Genocide in Hawaii* (1993), and Philip Curtin's *Death by Migration: Europe's Encounter with the Tropical World in the 19th Century* (1989) combine to show us two ways in which disease played radically different roles in the unfolding of nineteenth-century Western imperialism. Most recently, Edwin Fuller Torrey and Robert E. Yolken in *Beasts of the Earth: Animals, Humans and Disease* (2005) have combined to show us the ways in which the age-old interplay between human hosts and their animals has expedited the transmission and spread of disease – a theme only hinted at in McNeill's book.

FIGURE P.1 The First Horseman. Manuscript illumination of the first horseman, from the Burckhardt-Wildt Apocalypse, composed in England ca.1280.

Disease is, of course, much more than a distant historical phenomenon. It has been and remains, as John Aberth points out in this book, a constant force in human history that has had much more than just demographic repercussions. In the span of just two days, my local newspaper contained two items that remind us that the First Horseman of the Apocalypse, who kills by the deadly arrows of plague, still rides his white horse (Revelation 6:2).

The first article reported that the estimated number of living Americans with HIV now surpasses one million, reflecting both advances and failure in the ongoing fight against this deadly virus. New medicines and therapies currently allow infected victims to live longer, more productive lives than ever before, but the number of new annual infections, estimated to be at least 40,000, reflects a dismal social failure. As Aberth informs us, disease is much more than just a medical problem. It is a social construct that has cultural and societal origins, as well as cultural and societal defenses and consequences.

The second item, an editorial, reported that more than 100 health and emergency experts were meeting in Vermont, my home state, to conduct an eight-hour exercise simulating a crisis in which they had to respond to a global pandemic of avian flu(H_5N_1) out of East Asia that had already infected one-third of the state's population. This was not an empty academic exercise or play-acting to fill an otherwise boring day. Many experts, mindful of the Influenza Pandemic of 1918–1919 that killed upwards of 40 million people worldwide, fear that the next major pandemic might well be caused by a virus that has mutated out of avian influenza, a disease that has infected millions of birds in Asia and Eastern Europe and, more frighteningly, has managed to jump to a variety of mammals, including domestic cats. The good news is that, to date, only a few hundred humans are known to have been infected. The bad news is that 50 percent of them died.

To fail to be prepared for a rapid and effective response against such a threat would be foolish, irresponsible, and dangerous. More than 500,000 citizens of the USA have died as a result of three flu pandemics during the last century. The next one, and there will be another one, could be even more devastating, unless effective vaccines are produced and made available in sufficient quantities, and unless health officials have well-thought-out plans for coping with a large-scale medical emergency. And producing an effective flu vaccine is not a one-shot deal. Because of viruses' ability to mutate rapidly, medical researchers must develop new vaccine defenses on an annual basis, and governmental agencies and pharmaceutical companies must lend effective support in making it possible for those vaccines to be produced, stored, and distributed. One misstep, or one lost year, could spell disaster and death for many. It could even occasion an economic collapse of global proportions.

Complicating the challenge is the fact that developing and manufacturing effective vaccines and other anti-viral medications is costly to the point of being unprofitable for many pharmaceutical companies, and the chances of legal action from the almost inevitable side effects that some recipients will suffer only adds to the disincentive faced by the medical industry. This means that combating current and potential epidemics becomes a political problem that governments must grapple with. And, as Aberth demonstates in this book, this political face of disease is not unique to the twenty-first century.

In four case studies spanning more than 650 years, from the mid-fourteenth to the early twenty-first century, Aberth shows us the effects of bubonic and pneumonic plague (including the so-called Black Death), smallpox, and AIDS in such widely scattered areas of the world as Western Europe, the Middle East, the Americas, India, China, and sub-Saharan Africa. The deadly cast of characters is constantly changing, but the devastation and often (but not always) the human reactions, social consequences, and political responses are surprisingly similar.

This is not a book that one picks up for light reading. Its subject matter is grim, its stories often heartbreaking. Yet, it is an important book that should be read, mulled over, and discussed by students of world history at every level. If the study of world history has any utility, and we believe it does, then study of the manner in which diseases have ravaged human societies across the centuries and around the world and the ways that humans have responded to these crises should enable us not only to understand but to cope more wisely with the next epidemic that threatens our physical, psychological, and social well-being. Aberth perhaps expresses it best in the concluding words of this little book: "The history of disease will go on, despite once confident predictions of an end to epidemics in our times, and those who now wage the heroic struggle to find elusive cures to our new plagues may find that they have more to learn from the past than had once been thought."

Alfred J. Andrea
Series Editor

About the Author

John Aberth received his Ph.D. in Medieval History from the University of Cambridge in England and is the author of five books, including *The Black Death: The Great Mortality of 1348–1350*, and *From the Brink of the Apocalypse: Confronting Famine, War, Plague and Death in the Later Middle Ages*. He lives in Roxbury, Vermont.

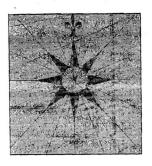

Introduction

THE TYPES AND CAUSES OF DISEASE

The history of disease is as old as, if not older than, the history of humankind, and the two are intimately intertwined. Ever since Paleolithic peoples emerged about half a million years ago, with the ability to make tools, hunt in groups, and live in communal shelters, they undoubtedly ingested a variety of microparasites from their food, water, and each other. But it is thought that their small numbers, relative isolation and nomadic existence kept disease in abeyance. It was not until our Neolithic ancestors began settlement patterns around 8000 B.C.E. that disease played a regular and enduring role in human history. The domestication and close contact with animals, rapid increase in numbers, the attendant accumulation of refuse and human waste, and the creation of irrigation and stagnant water supplies all facilitated the introduction and spread of disease organisms. When disease became permanently established in an animal or human population, it was

endemic. From time to time, an outbreak of the disease would erupt and prevail among large numbers of the community, in which case it was an **epidemic**. When civilizations began to practice trade and commerce with each other after the development of better transportation techniques, such as the invention of the wagon wheel about 3000 B.C.E., it was now possible for a disease to become **pandemic** as it spread across large geographical areas from one society to another.

The number and kind of epidemic and pandemic disease outbreaks that have appeared on the stage of human history are legion. Broadly speaking, we can divide diseases by the microorganisms responsible: the vast majority of illnesses being caused by either a **bacterium** or a **virus**. Bacteria are one-celled microorganisms that invade the body and rapidly begin reproducing, thus creating the disease condition; they usually can be fought with **antibiotics** that kill the bacteria outright or with **vaccines** that create antibodies against the bacterial antigens. Viruses are not complete organisms like bacteria, but must attach themselves to cells in order to reproduce their nucleic acid by introducing it into the cell through its protective protein coat. So far, the only defense against viruses seems to be to create vaccines using harmless replicas, such as the cowpox virus, which provides immunity against smallpox, or using a "killed-virus" in which its nucleic acid has been inactivated. Diseases caused by bacteria include plague, pneumonia, anthrax, cholera, tuberculosis, brucellosis, leprosy, scrofula, syphilis, gonorrhea, erysipelas, scarlet fever, meningitis, diphtheria, dysentery, and typhoid fever; those caused by viruses include smallpox, measles, influenza, poliomyelitis, herpes, hepatitis, AIDS (acquired immunodeficiency syndrome), Ebola and other hemorrhagic fevers, SARS (severe acute respiratory syndrome), yellow fever, dengue fever, mumps, and rubella. Ergotism, also known as St. Anthony's Fire, is an example of a disease caused by a mold or fungus, while some diseases are induced by unique microorganisms that fall into none of the above categories; these include typhus (caused by *Rickettsia*), malaria (caused by a plasmodium), and African typanosomiasis, or sleeping sickness (caused by a trypanosome). Typically, diseases are communicated by bodily fluids, food or water supplies, or by insect vectors, such as mosquitos (malaria and yellow fever), fleas (bubonic plague), lice (typhus), flies (sleeping sickness), and ticks (Lyme disease and tularemia). There are also illnesses caused by the ingestion of multi-celled parasites, such as the worms responsible for schistosomiasis, or bilharzia, and trichinosis. Then there are disease conditions caused by deficiencies in human diet or behavior, such as anemia (lack of iron), pellagra (lack of niacin), beriberi (lack of thiamine), scurvy (lack of vitamin C), rickets (lack of vitamin D), ophthalmia (lack of vitamin A), osteoporosis (lack of calcium), along with cirrhosis, diabetes, emphysema, dropsy and anorexia. Finally, there are some illnesses, both historic and current, that have mysterious causes little understood, even today; these include cancer, epilepsy, arthritis, heart disease, gout, Alzheimer's disease, Parkinson's disease, the sweating sickness, chlorosis, tarantism, and Creutzfeldt-Jakob disease (known in animals as bovine spongiform encephapathology, or mad cow disease).

THE IMPACT OF DISEASE

All these diseases, of course, vary greatly in their **morbidity**, or incidence among a given population, and in their **mortality**, or death rate, factors that have determined the extent of their role in history. Some, such as plague or smallpox, are infamous for their high morbidity and mortality, which at certain times and places have exceeded 50 percent. Others, such as leprosy or syphilis, are far less infectious and rarely fatal, at least in the short term, but nonetheless these diseases can be chronic in nature and serve as significant "background noise" in people's lives. The situation can be complicated by the fact that the bacterium or virus may change over time and thus alter its epidemiological behavior. Often this is a mutually adaptive process in which the organism or submicroscopic entity becomes progressively less deadly in a population repeatedly exposed to it, to the point that it becomes a "childhood disease," as happened in the West with measles and varicella (chickenpox). In some cases, modern medicine has intervened to effectively eradicate the historical existence of epidemics, as happened to syphilis, pneumonia, and plague due to penicillin developed by Alexander Fleming in the first half of the twentieth century; smallpox after Edward Jenner's cowpox vaccine in the late eighteenth century; and polio as a result of vaccines formulated by Jonas Salk and Albert Sabin in the mid-twentieth century. But other diseases, though they have emerged in modern times when their victims are armed with sophisticated diagnostic techniques and a wide array of powerful drugs, continue to elude prevention or cure. One of the reasons that no vaccine has been found to date for AIDS, for example, is that the human immunodeficiency virus (HIV) that causes the disease is highly mutable, and thus presents an elusive target for treatment. And there are older diseases, such as tuberculosis, influenza, and malaria, that once were thought to be conquerable but recently have revived to wreak their havoc yet again on the world stage.

The modern age of medicine, which could be said to have dawned in the second half of the nineteenth century, brought with it the powerful knowledge that microscopic germs are at the root of many illnesses that plagued humankind throughout its history. As pioneered by a French chemist, Louis Pasteur, and his German colleague, Robert Koch, the emerging field of bacteriology opened a new chapter in the approach to and study of disease. On occasion, biologists have been lucky enough to extract microorganisms from the graves they share with their hosts. In 2000, a French team was able to recover the DNA of *Yersinia pestis*, the bacterium thought responsible for the Black Death outbreak in Europe and the Middle East during the late Middle Ages, from the dental pulp of some fourteenth-century plague victims in Montpellier, France. Medical historians are sometimes also able to use modern evolutionary theory and recent disease outbreaks in isolated, nonimmune populations to establish a model for how disease would have affected our ancestors. By and large, however, we are left to fall back on the simple but careful study of two types of physical evidence left behind by those who lived and died through the disease outbreaks we seek to reconstruct: skeletal and mummified remains of victims, and the writings of physicians, chroniclers and others who observed the disease.

DISEASE AND THE HISTORIAN

Examination of skeletal and mummified remains have proved especially useful for reconstructing the disease epidemics that afflicted prehistoric humans and populations on the American and African continents, where written records are mostly unavailable prior to the intrusion of Europeans. Diseases that leave detectable traces on human bone include arthritis, dental decay, anemia, tumors, treponematosis (a family of venereal illnesses that includes syphilis and yaws), tuberculosis, and dietary deficiencies. These are usually expressed as bone lesions or deformities visible to the naked eye of the trained observer. Mummified organs and other bodily parts can reveal the existence of influenza, pneumonia, trichinosis, tuberculosis, and leishmaniasis.

Certainly the more accessible and prolific source, which forms the basis of this book, is the written record. For Europe and the Middle East, the foundation of pre-modern medical literature was laid by Hippocrates of Cos (ca.460–ca.377 B.C.E.) and Galen of Pergamum (ca.130–ca.210 C.E.), along with the traditional corpus of works that grew up around them. Advancing a rational explanation for human disease – as opposed to a magical or divine causation – which in turn presupposed that illness could be cured or ameliorated by human agency alone was a signal achievement of these men. Even though the miasmatic and humoral theories of disease agency – that sickness spreads through a corruption of the air, which upsets the balance of the four humors once it enters the body – may seem little better than superstition to the minds of modern students, it was the shift in attitudes rather than results that was the most lasting legacy of ancient Greek and Roman medicine. A scientific approach could now be tendered toward a whole host of diseases, such as apoplexy, asthma, bubonic plague, cancer, diphtheria, dysentery, epilepsy, erysipelas, and malaria, all of which were studied and described by the Hippocratic and Galenic schools. From the ninth to the twelfth centuries, this ancient medical tradition was re-discovered, and even improved upon, by Arabic authors such as Rhazes (al-Razi), Avicenna (Ibn Sina), Averroes (Ibn Rushd), and Avenzoar (Ibn Zuhr), whose treatises were translated and transmitted to western Europe by the thirteenth century. Added to this, we have numerous accounts of significant disease outbreaks by non-medical authors, such as chroniclers, annalists, and historians. The most famous of these include the description of the "Plague of Athens" of 430–426 B.C.E. (perhaps smallpox or typhus) by Thucydides and of the "Plague of Justinian" of 542 C.E. (undoubtedly bubonic plague) by Procopius of Caesarea. By the time we reach the Black Death during the fourteenth and fifteenth centuries, the number of authors has multiplied to the point that comparative evaluations of sources on a single disease outbreak can now be made.

The written medical tradition from China and India is just as ancient and distinguished as in the West. The *Huangdi Nei Jing* (*The Yellow Emperor's Classic of Medicine*), dating to the first century B.C.E., diagnoses diseases according to a sixfold classification system that is comparable to the fourfold humoral system of the Greeks. Even older texts, all dating to the Zhou Dynasty from the eighth to the fifth centuries B.C.E., likewise discuss disease in technical terms. In India, Ayurvedic (the art of prolonging life) texts from the sixth century

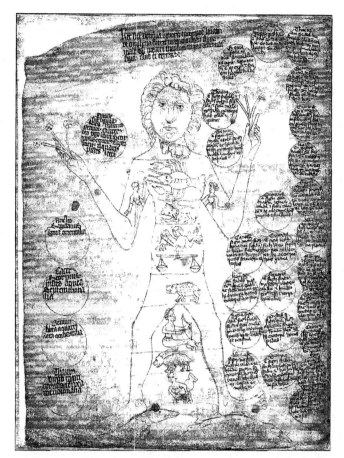

FIGURE I.1 Medieval Medicine.   A medieval drawing of a naked man with the twelve signs of the zodiac placed in corresponding parts of his anatomy. The sign indicated the most advantageous time when each part of the body could be cured. From an encyclopedic medical manuscript from South Germany, ca.1410.

B.C.E. discuss the balance of the three *dosas*, or bodily essences, as essential to health, in a system once again remarkably similar to the humoral theory of the ancient West. Rickets, beriberi, pneumonia, influenza, cirrhosis, malaria, tuberculosis, leprosy, and cholera were all diseases that seem to have been diagnosed by the ancient Chinese and Indians, based on their descriptions of symptoms.

In terms of modern historical writing about disease, two major trends may be discerned. First, disease came to be seen as playing a decisive and deterministic role in history: affecting the outcome of wars,

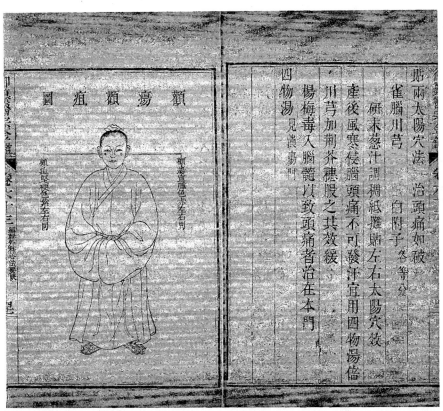

FIGURE I.2 Chinese Herbal Medicine. An illustration of the proper usage for Chinese herbal medicine for illnesses, from the *Yizong Jinjian* (*Complete Survey of Medical Knowledge*), printed in Beijing in 1743.

cutting short the reigns of kings and queens, forcing the modification of traditional institutions and customs, even deciding the fate of whole civilizations and peoples. Disease was therefore now regarded as an **exogenous** factor acting upon human history, an impersonal, inexorable force of change that obeyed its own laws and rhythms regardless of the character and make-up of any particular society, rather on a par with how Marxism explains history through the concept of class conflict. At nearly the same time, however, a second, parallel trend emerged that saw disease as an **endogenous** variable: a social or cultural construct in which the illness could be defined solely in terms of the preconceptions and circumstances operating within a society at any given point in time. To take but one example, ADD, or attention deficit disorder, is an adolescent condition that is today widely recognized and familiar to doctors, teachers, and parents, for which drugs are prescribed and special needs identified. But prior to the 1980s, children suffering from ADD would have been classified as simply misbehaved, rather than as victims of a personality disorder, and the same could be said for any number of currently diagnosed mental conditions. Carrying such an argument to its extreme, one historian has theorized that skin freckles could one day be classified as a disease, should a sufficient consensus in society deem it justified to do so, complete with a "National Institute of Freckle Research." This "relativist" approach to illness contrasts with an older, "positivist" school that defined disease more narrowly as the result of specific biological processes that arose when foreign or "abnormal stimuli" were introduced into a host organism.

Neither of these trends in the historical study of disease is entirely new. Both Thucydides and Procopius, for example, clearly recognized that their plagues played a crucial role in the course of the Peloponnesian War and the Wars of Justinian, respectively, and both chronicled the social consequences of disease, particularly with regard to nursing and burial of the dead and dying, which served as a model for later generations of writers. But it could fairly be said that the reformulation of these debates in recent decades has reinvigorated the field of the history of disease and medicine, both in terms of the sheer number of such studies and in terms of their reach into other disciplines. Nor, most recently, have the revisionists themselves been immune from revision. When William McNeill published his landmark study, *Plagues and Peoples*, in 1976, he based his thesis of disease as an exogenous, and largely destructive, actor on the stage of human history upon two main disease episodes: the Black Death in Europe and the Middle East during the late Middle Ages, and the arrival of smallpox and other ills from Europe to the New World during the early modern era. But McNeill's view has now been taken to task for failing to account for endogenous variables that could alter the course of disease's role in human affairs: in the case of the Black Death, it has been argued that Europeans greatly mollified, and even turned to good account, the disease's impact upon society through fertility responses, sanitation and public health measures, and technological advances. In the case of smallpox's devastation in the Americas, the fact that disease coincided with European colonialism – in particular, the collective impact of Spanish oppression of natives, commonly referred to as the "Black Legend" – greatly affected the way in which disease exerted its deadly influence. By the same token, relativists' approach to disease as a social construct has lately been criticized as giving too little weight to the absolute reality that some diseases exist through their biological aspects alone, regardless of how society views them. A new history of disease that would instead combine and integrate both approaches – the relativist and the positivist – has lately been proposed. As we will see in Chapter 4, this debate has been played out with particular intensity in the case of AIDS.

On a final note, one must observe another general trend in disease historiography, namely the profound loss of confidence among historians and other observers that the history of disease will ever end. In contrast to an earlier age, coinciding with the heyday of bacteriology, that predicted the "end of epidemics" and chronicled disease history as one of inexorable "conquest" by human researchers, we now find, almost without exception, the view that the horizon of humankind's struggle with disease stretches infinitely into the future. Indeed, with the multitude of new and as yet incurable "plagues" now on the scene – AIDS, SARS, Ebola, hantavirus, mad cow disease, and avian flu, to name but a few examples – an almost hysterical alarm has been rung that our disease history is about to get much worse.

THE SPREAD OF DISEASES

One of the purposes of this series is to demonstrate the temporal and geographical scope of selected topics, and this is certainly true of disease. As already indicated, the disease condition has been around probably for as long as the earth has been in existence, and the relevance of disease has by no means diminished in the modern era with the advent of advanced medical knowledge and techniques, despite premature predictions to the contrary. Geographically speaking, some diseases are naturally endemic to certain regions, where they seem, in fact, to have originated. Thus, India may be the ancestral home of cholera, Africa of AIDS (albeit this origin is contested), and the Americas of syphilis. Yet it would be a mistake to think that any disease is confined to any part of the world. Since time immemorial, malaria has appeared wherever there are breeding grounds for its mosquito vector, whether these be the swamps of Rome or the jungles of equatorial Africa. Smallpox appears to have ancient origins in Europe, China, and India. Bubonic plague may have come to the Mediterranean from several endemic centers–in sub-Saharan Africa, Central Asia, or northeastern India. Geographical barriers to disease become meaningless when large-scale trade and travel succeed in connecting far-flung places of the world. The Mongol Empire made possible the Black Death during the mid-fourteenth century that swept away millions in Europe and Southwest Asia in two short years, while the discovery of the Americas by European explorers beginning in the 1490s set in train a host of epidemics that over the next two centuries decimated the native population in what has been described as a disease "holocaust". But it was the advent of steamship travel in the nineteenth century and airplane travel in the twentieth that inaugurated worldwide pandemics, now made possible by the quick and efficient transport of pathogens in their animal and human passengers. A disease that was once exotic in a far corner of the globe could now be your neighborhood scourge. This new reality was amply demonstrated by the Influenza Pandemic of 1918–1919, which is estimated to have killed at least 30 million people worldwide. AIDS is the latest plague that has proven itself capable of pandemic proportions, and it undoubtedly will be joined by many more. West Nile fever, SARS, and avian flu are the latest imports into the Western hemisphere from abroad, which so far have narrowly averted becoming full-blown epidemics through the precautions set in place against global terrorism.

DISEASE AND SOCIETY

Another goal of the *Connections* series is to show the interdisciplinary nature of its topics, and disease assuredly lends itself to such connections. Several historians have recently explored how disease went hand in hand with imperialism, especially as practiced by the European powers during the nineteenth century, and Chapter 3 showcases this connection. Trade was an especially vital conduit of the Black Death (Chapter 1), while religious and cultural conflicts played leading roles in the advent and spread of smallpox in the New World (Chapter 2). Finally, the age-old dichotomy between science (including medicine) and faith is currently being played out most dramatically in the AIDS crisis in Africa (Chapter 4). But all of these themes, as well as many others, can be found in each of the case studies explored in the following chapters.

CHAPTER

1

A Eurasian Pandemic: The Black Death in Europe and the Middle East, 1347–1350

THE ORIGINS OF THE BLACK DEATH

The disease known as the Black Death first came to Europe, according to the Sicilian chronicler, Michele da Piazza, in October 1347, when the port of Messina on the northeastern tip of the island hosted twelve Genoese galleys whose sailors "brought with them a plague that they carried down to the very marrow of their bones." Landing almost simultaneously at other major trading ports in Italy and southern France, the Black Death began its terror in earnest in 1348, when the disease spread throughout Italy, France, and Spain, and invaded Switzerland, Austria, England, and perhaps Denmark. In the eastern Mediterranean, plague seems to have pursued a similar course, first coming to Constantinople in the spring of 1347 and then to Alexandria in Egypt by the end of that year; from these two major ports, the disease spread throughout the Aegean, the Balkans, Palestine, Syria, and the North African coast by the spring and summer of 1348. Thereafter, in 1349 and 1350, plague came to all of Germany and eastern Europe, to the Low Countries, all of the British Isles, and all of Scandinavia. While the silence of the records indicates that it skipped over Poland and Bohemia, plague finally arrived in Russia (probably by way of Sweden) in 1352.

The Black Death probably originated in Central Asia, in the heart of the Mongol Empire, and spread westward along overland trade routes to the Crimea on the north coast of the Black Sea, where it made its first contact with European (mostly Italian) merchants. A well-informed Muslim writing from Aleppo in northern Syria, Ibn al-Wardi, states that the plague began in "the land of darkness," where it had been present for 15 years, or since 1331–1332. Since by al-Wardi's account, the disease invaded China and India subsequent to these origins, it seems clear that the region referred to is that area of Inner Asia known as Mongolia, whose inhabitants, the Mongols, had been for nearly a century the most hated and feared enemy of the Mamluk dynasty that ruled al-Wardi's native Syria. A Florentine chronicler, Giovanni Villani, confirms that the plague was very virulent among the "Tartars," or Mongols, while another Muslim author, al-Maqrizi of Cairo, Egypt, reports that in 1341 the plague began "in the land of the Great Khan, . . . a country inhabited by the Khitai [a non-Chinese people who once ruled northern China] and the Mongols." Although Maqrizi wrote in the fifteenth century, he perhaps based his history on earlier sources, and in this instance he says his information came from "the land of the Uzbek [Uzbekistan in Central Asia]." Added to this is archaeological evidence uncovered in 1885 of ten plague victims recorded in 1338–1339 on three Nestorian Christian headstones in present-day Kyrgyzstan. Modern epidemiological studies suggest that the plague bacillus is endemic in the rodent populations of the Central Asian steppes, where it may have become established by the fourteenth century after Mongol armies had brought it there from an even older reservoir in the Himalayan foothills.

The immediate launching point for the plague's arrival in Europe was the Black Sea region, which had known a Genoese presence from the second half of the thirteenth century, when the Mongol rulers of the Golden Horde were fostering trade with the West. At the same time, the Genoese were granted access to the Black Sea by the Byzantine emperor. Thus, Genoa and other Italian cities established their commercial agents at Caffa, Tana [Azov], and other cities along

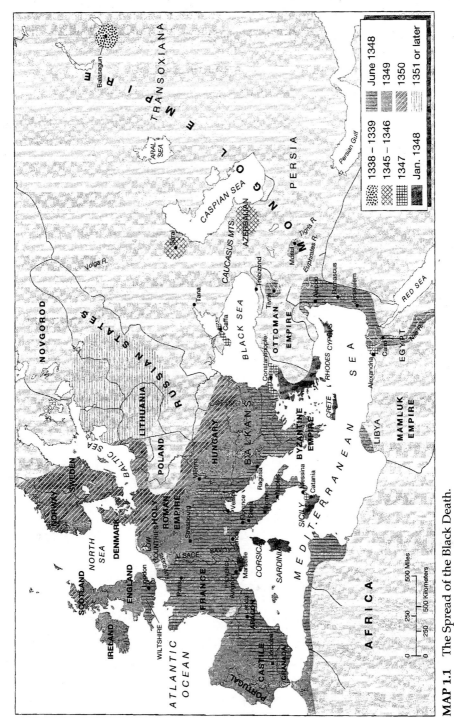

MAP 1.1 The Spread of the Black Death.

Legend:

1338 – 1339
1345 – 1346
1347
Jan. 1348
June 1348
1349
1350
1351 or later

the northern coast. Their galleys and sailing vessels loaded up with local products such as grain, alum, slaves, and above all, expensive animal furs, including ermine and marten. The last commodity could have carried bubonic plague-bearing fleas, allowing the disease to come on board ship. A rather more dramatic story of the first plague contact between Asians and Europeans is told by the Piacenzan chronicler, Gabriele de Mussis: A plague-stricken Mongol army called off its siege of Genoese merchants in Caffa (present-day Feodosiya) in 1346, but not before they had "ordered that their cadavers be placed on their catapults and lobbed into the city of Caffa in order that the intolerable stench of those bodies might extinguish everyone [inside]." It is to be wondered, though, whether bubonic plague-bearing fleas could survive being catapulted toward new human hosts, as a kind of medieval germ warfare. Whatever the means of transmission, plague-bearing cargo – be it insect, animal, or human – introduced the disease to Europe. While the journey from Caffa to Genoa was long – no less than 2,200 miles that took anywhere from one to three months – these ships still could have communicated plague even after the disease had run its course through the rat and human populations on board. Rat fleas can survive up to 80 days without a host, and the bacillus itself can survive up to 5 weeks in the fleas' feces. Also, the distance and thus time for incubation could be considerably shortened if the Italians were bringing the plague back from their colonies and trading posts in the Aegean and the Balkans, rather than all the way from the Black Sea. An elaborate, extensive network of sea and land routes then carried the disease throughout the continent.

Although modern students and historians automatically refer to this epidemiological phenomenon as the "Black Death," the medieval men and women who experienced the disease never called it by this name. Instead, contemporary accounts most commonly speak of the "pestilence," the "plague" (from the Latin word, *plaga*, meaning "a blow"), or the "great mortality." The term "Black Death" was first coined by Scandinavian chroniclers in the sixteenth century and popularized by German and English historians in the nineteenth century. Even so, the "Black Death" is now the standard designation for this specific historical event, the so-called Second Pandemic of a disease that wiped out roughly half of Europe's population in a little over two years. The First Pandemic of plague afflicted the Mediterranean region between 542 and 750 C.E., while the Third Pandemic struck mainly India and China between 1894 and 1930 (see Chapter 3). The plague of 1347–1350, and its many subsequent outbreaks throughout the second half of the fourteenth century and throughout the fifteenth century, is considered by many historians to be the defining event of the late Middle Ages, one that brought in its train a whole host of seismic impacts upon society and culture.

WHAT WAS THE BLACK DEATH?

Identification of the causative organism behind plague is usually credited to a French microbiologist, Alexandre Yersin, after whom the bacterium *Yersinia pestis* is named and who carried out his studies during a plague outbreak in Hong Kong in 1894. As plague continued to ravage parts of India and China well into the twentieth century, other scientists gained a unique opportunity to study the transmission and symptoms of the disease. Based on modern observations, we know that plague appears in three forms, depending on how the bacterium invades the body. The most common form, called bubonic plague, spreads the bacteria through the bite of a flea, whose upper stomach becomes blocked by the rapidly-multiplying microorganisms and thus will constantly feed and regurgitate bacteria into the bloodstream of its hosts. Once its usual animal carriers have grown dead and cold, fleas will jump onto the nearest warm body available, including humans. From the time of infection, incubation of the plague bacilli in the human bloodstream may take two days to a week before symptoms appear. The most notable symptom is, of course, one or more painful swellings of the lymph nodes, known as buboes, in the region of the armpits, neck, or, most frequently, in the groin, depending on where the fleas have initially infected the victim. This may be accompanied by high fever, headaches, internal bleeding just below the skin, vomiting, delirium or stupor, and loss of motor control. Death typically ensues within 3–6 days after the onset of symptoms. But approximately 10–40 percent of the victims of bubonic plague survive without medical intervention: A sign of their recovery is that, early in the second week of symptoms, their buboes burst and release pus.

There are other, even more deadly forms of the disease. In pneumonic plague, the bacteria are communicated through respiratory fluids, much like the common cold, which allows the disease to spread rapidly and efficiently. Once it invades the lungs, this form produces a bloody sputum and typically kills within 2–3 days in nearly 100 percent of its victims. Septicemic plague, the most mysterious and rare form, seems to spread through a direct invasion, or "poisoning," of the blood, perhaps as the result of tainted medical instruments or the bite of a human flea, *Pulex irritans*, both of which could directly transfer the plague bacteria from the bloodstream of one patient to another. This form of the plague is also universally lethal, and it can apparently kill within hours. The Black Death is now cured by penicillin, or any number of antibiotic substitutes, provided that the disease is diagnosed before its advanced stages. Such medicines, of course, were not available in the fourteenth century.

Some scholars have questioned whether the Black Death should be identified with the modern disease known as plague. Objections have been raised on a variety of grounds, including whether the biology of the rat–flea nexus could support such a wide-ranging and fast-spreading epidemic, and, most recently, a claim of lack of concurrence of symptoms, seasonality, morbidity, and other epidemiological factors between the two incidents of the disease. However, none of the objections is itself ironclad, and even if successful in challenging plague, they still leave open the question, what is to take its place? So far, any likely alternatives face equal, if not greater, difficulties of explanation. One answer to the mystery may be that the DNA of the plague bacterium is able to mutate into "hypervirulent" strains that behave differently than normal, and in fact such "atypical" plague bacilli do occur regularly in nature. In the end, it is perhaps irrelevant that we positively identify the Black Death with any given disease; whatever it was, it killed an awful lot of people.

THE BLACK DEATH AS A SOCIAL FORCE

A more burning question for students and historians is to explain the Black Death as an historical event. By almost any measure, the Black Death is considered by most scholars to be a watershed event in history due to the timing, geography, and extent of its appearance on the Eurasian world stage. The disease struck at a time when Europe had not known an outbreak of plague for many centuries, possibly not since the years between 542 and 750 c.e., when the "Plague of Justinian" ravaged the Mediterranean region. Although a "Great Famine" struck northern Europe between 1315 and 1322, nothing prepared Europeans for the horrendous onslaught of the Black Death. If genetic or biological immunity to the disease is possible, they had as yet not acquired it, let alone social, economic, or psychological defenses. Thus, the initial shock that the plague caused throughout Europe between 1347 and 1350 should not be discounted. Many chroniclers turned to apocalyptic language in order to describe the Black Death's awesome impact. Agnolo di Tura of Siena, for example, baldly stated that in 1348, "so many have died that everyone believes it is the end of the world." Writing from Avignon, Louis Sanctus described the origins of the plague in India in 1347 as a rain of thunder, lightning, hail, fire, and smoke, all of which is highly reminiscent of the seven angels about to blow their seven trumpets in Chapter 8 of the Book of Revelation. Likewise, Gabriele de Mussis of Piacenza compared the irruption of plague boils to the "fiery seals" produced by the seven angels pouring out the seven bowls of God's wrath in Chapter 16. While such millennial expectations were not fulfilled, the Black Death did return, albeit with considerably less virulence, almost once a decade throughout the second half of the fourteenth century and at least the first half of the fifteenth century. The plague and other diseases kept Europe's population stagnant or even slightly in decline until the dawn of the early modern period.

THE SPREAD OF THE BLACK DEATH

The great mortality of 1348 was also wide ranging in its geographical incidence. Every country and region in Europe was affected, with the probable exception of Poland and Bohemia, whose relative isolation from mercantile contacts possibly spared them the disease. The Black Death was therefore a shared experience among medieval Europeans in a way that no other event could match, producing a remarkably similar set of responses and explanations. It also made some European chroniclers fully aware that they were part of a worldwide phenomenon, which embraced neighboring regions such as the Middle East and the Black Sea, as well as lands far to the East, in India and China. The plague probably began as an endemic, that is, a locally confined disease that, once established, was to be perpetually present in a given area. Such endemics seem to have existed in the Himalayan foothills and the Eurasian steppes, where the plague bacillus could survive indefinitely in the warm burrows of the native marmot rodents. It then became pandemic when the flea, rodent, or human populations spread the disease far afield through faster, more efficient trade or communication networks newly made available. This very situation arose by the second half of the thirteenth century through the establishment of the far-flung Mongol Empire. As experienced by Marco Polo and other intrepid travelers, the Mongols linked Asia to Europe in an overland network of mounted armies, postal carriers, and caravans. Once transmitted from its endemic centers in the East, the plague easily made its way across Eurasia through trade links that had been established throughout the Mediterranean and Black Sea regions during the previous era of the Crusades.

THE MORTALITY RATE OF THE BLACK DEATH

Finally, the Black Death was unusually potent in the human mortality it caused. Previously, the prevailing view among modern scholars of the plague was (and to some extent still is) that the disease carried off roughly a third of Europe's inhabitants during its first and most devastating outbreak in 1348. This estimate is too low and must be revised upwards in light of new research on plague demography. The latest evidence points to an *average* mortality rate of at least 50 percent, or half the population succumbing to the disease. English episcopal registers, which record deaths among the parish clergy within a bishop's diocese and are among the most accurate of contemporary documents available, yield a mean mortality rate of 45 percent. Manorial records, which also survive in plentiful supply from England and which register the deaths of a lord's tenants, usually through the payment of death taxes, all point to death rates between 40 and 70 percent. On the Continent, although fewer records survive than in England, a variety of documents including parish registers, tax assessments, household census returns, scribal records, and episcopal registers from France, Italy, and Spain record mortalities from the plague ranging from 45 to 68 percent. A 50 percent average mortality rate also would be more in line with what contemporary chroniclers had to say of the Black Death. Admittedly, medieval authors were prone to exaggeration – Giovanni Boccaccio, for instance, reported 100,000 dead in Florence, when the city probably contained no more than 80,000 souls. But while medieval numerical estimates must always be approached with caution, they nonetheless testify to the perceived severity of the disease.

A TURNING POINT IN HISTORY?

Given the large number of deaths, it is not surprising that modern historians traditionally have seen the Black Death as playing a pivotal role in late medieval society. Yet this was not always the case: A little over 30 years ago, a new view emerged when a collection of essays was published under the title *The Black Death: A Turning Point in History?* The question mark in the title is significant, for it implies that the Black Death's pivotal role in late medieval society, which had been assumed by an older generation of scholars, was now being challenged. Arguing on the basis of neo-Malthusian economics, revisionist historians recast the Black Death as a necessary and long-overdue corrective to an overpopulated Europe; in this view, then, the disease was not a sudden and violent irruption but an inevitable consequence of a medieval population that had outgrown its agricultural capacity to feed itself.

Most recently, post-revisionist historians have been swinging the pendulum back toward restoring the Black Death as, indeed, a turning point, or watershed, in late medieval history. In contrast to portraying medieval humans as helpless pawns in the grip of economic forces beyond their control, these historians point out that even in the Middle Ages, people had the power to help change their destiny, for good or ill; they expressed this power, for example, in their decisions about marriages and births in response to the mortality created by numerous visitations of the plague. But although the Black Death has been restored to its place as a transforming event, it is one that is now seen as having had an overall positive rather than negative impact upon society. Its silver lining was that it forced Europeans (but not, apparently, Middle Easterners) to make technological innovations and changes that helped usher in the modern era. Labor shortages created by successive bouts of plague may have impelled the use of more efficient agricultural techniques and the introduction of better machines of manufacture, such as the printing press. A dearth of men may have created more working opportunities for women, especially in towns, and a "cult of remembrance" that sprang up after the plague may have helped spawn secular patronage of Renaissance art. Declining mortalities from successive plagues as a result of increased immunity may have given physicians the confidence to adopt a more empirical approach to medicine. On the other hand, one is also impressed by the remarkable resilience of late medieval culture and religion in the face of a catastrophe with the cataclysmic power to topple civilizations. The ability of plague survivors to recover and re-invigorate their time-honored customs and beliefs allowed for a great deal of continuity and a more gradual transition than the artificial dividing lines between medieval and early modern suggest.

CONTEMPORARY VIEWS OF THE BLACK DEATH

How did contemporaries view the Black Death? As might be expected, their explanations of the disease often invoked the agency of God, for whom the plague was an instrument of almighty wrath wreaked upon humanity in retribution for its wickedness and sin. The "scientific" interpretation of the plague was no less indebted to tradition and authority. One medical writer after another deferred to the ancient legacy of Hippocrates and Galen, which taught that epidemic disease was spread through a miasma, or harmful corruption of the air, but which did not preclude the possibility of direct, victim-to-victim contagion. For cures, medieval doctors followed the ancients in prescribing phlebotomies, or bleeding of the patient, in order to restore the balance of the body's four humors, as well as ingestion of a theriac, a special syrupy concoction containing dozens of exotic ingredients designed to neutralize the foreign poison thought to be causing the disease. But a few physicians, such Ibn Khatima of Almería in Spain, Gui de Chauliac, physician to the pope in Avignon, and Gentile da Foligno of the University of Padua, recognized that the Black Death was an unprecedented disease unknown even to the ancients and may have begun to rely on their own experience in treating it. Some preventative measures that doctors prescribed, such as flight from and quarantine of an infected area, fumigation of the home, or clearing of refuse, would have had a practical and beneficial effect and were adopted by the health boards set up by some cities to combat the plague (see Figure 1.1).

FIGURE 1.1 Plague Burial. Survivors burying the dead in coffins, as mandated by city ordinance, during the Black Death at Tournai in Flanders in 1349. From a late medieval manuscript copy of the *Chronicle* of Gilles li Muisis.

THE IMPACT OF THE BLACK DEATH

The varied impact that the Black Death had upon late medieval society was well noted by contemporaries. In social terms, chronicler after chronicler recorded the devastating effect that the plague had upon even the closest of family ties. That "brothers abandoned brothers," husbands their wives, and parents even their own children is a refrain heard again and again in the plague chronicles. Another oft-repeated complaint is that traditional mores and values began to break down in the wake of the Black Death, as people cast aside all fear of breaking the rules in the face of rampant mortality. Of course, descriptions of "shell shock" among a catastrophe's survivors were a stock in trade of historical writing going all the way back to Thucydides' famous account of the Plague of Athens in 430–426 B.C.E. Therefore, it is hard to tell how genuine such stereotypical characterizations are of true social behavior in time of plague.

Economically, observers like Henry Knighton, canon of Leicester Abbey in England, and al-Maqrizi of Egypt testify that, in the immediate aftermath of 1348, the excessive mortality created a shortage of both producers and consumers, with the overall effect that wages of agricultural laborers went up and prices of goods went down, a situation that heralded higher living standards for serfs but lower manorial incomes for their lords. Although prices were to subsequently rise in the ensuing decades, according to English manorial records, laborers also learned to demand more and better food along with their wages. Aside from giving in completely to the competitive hiring of labor created by the post-plague shortages, landlords could either emancipate their serfs from their age-old labor services in return for money rents, in effect abandoning direct farming for the fixed income to be had from sharecroppers, or attempt to turn back the economic clock to before the Black Death. The latter alternative was tried by some city-states in Italy and the national governments of England, France, and Spain in the form of labor laws that set wages and prices to pre-plague levels and compelled idle workers to hire themselves out at the specified rates. Such legislation, of course, was well-nigh unenforceable, but the legal rolls that survive from fourteenth-century England are filled with prosecutions of offenders. Peasant revolts, such as those that took place in France in 1358, in Florence in 1378, and in London in 1381, testify to the tensions that this medieval version of a command economy could create in a post-plague society. By the fifteenth century, successive bouts of the plague had proven that the former solution – commutation of serfs into renters – was the only realistic alternative in the long term. Nonetheless, downward population pressures equally as great as Europe's do not seem to have led to liberation of the *fellaheen* peasant laborers in Egypt.

As already noted, for most European Christians, the extraordinary mortality of the Black Death was proof of the righteous judgment of God visited upon a sinful humanity. Religious appeals were directed to God and his saints who were especially known for their mercy or power against the plague, such as the Virgin Mary, St. Sebastian, St. Anthony, and St. Roch. Yet a number of sources also criticize the secular clergy, or priesthood, for failing to administer to the needs of parishioners during the Black Death, which would include hearing confession and giving last rites. Perhaps the harshest critics were the clergymen themselves. In a famous decree issued on January 10, 1349, Bishop Ralph Shrewsbury of Bath and Wells in England granted an unprecedented indulgence to the parishioners of his diocese to confess to a layman, even a woman, on the grounds that "many, we hear, are dying without the sacrament of penance" in parishes decimated by the plague because "priests cannot be found to take on the cares of these places, neither out of devotional zeal nor for payment, or to visit the sick and administer the church sacraments to them, perhaps because they are infected or have a fear of being infected." The archbishop of Canterbury, Simon Islip, castigated the clergy of his province for abandoning their parishes, blaming such behavior not on fear of contagion, but on the clerics' greed for richer livings, particularly private chantries where a wealthy patron paid to have masses said for the souls of himself and his family. However, one must remember that many more priests faithfully carried out their duties, judging from the mortality rate within the order, which in England averaged 45 percent among ten dioceses scattered throughout the country. In the diocese of Barcelona in Spain, mortality was even higher, reaching 60 percent in the year between May 1348 and April 1349. One also can make excuses for those priests who survived the plague and who could expect much lower incomes in offerings and tithes due from a flock ravaged by the Black Death. In these circumstances, the quest for supplemental funds from private masses becomes understandable rather than censorious.

Nevertheless, there was a religious movement during the Black Death that seemed to challenge the sacramental authority of the secular clergy. Although the evidence of wills, particularly from England, indicates that most parishioners remained rather conventional in their piety in the wake of the plague, a remarkable outpouring of collective guilt occurred during the years 1348 to 1350. This was the processional phenomenon of the flagellants, who got their name from the *flagella*, or whips, used in penitential ceremonies. The movement began in late 1348 in Austria or Hungary, and progressed from there to Thuringia and Franconia in central Germany by the spring of 1349. At that time, the movement is thought to have entered its most radical, and possibly heretical, phase, when it may have challenged the sacramental authority of priests to administer confession and penance, since flagellants were already performing this obligation to an excessive degree. Thereafter, it came to south Germany and the Rhineland that summer and continued on up to the Low Countries, where it persisted until the autumn of 1349, when Pope Clement VI and King Philip VI of France determined to suppress it. Given the prevalent belief that the plague was a righteous scourge sent down by God in retribution for man's wickedness and sin, it was perfectly logical to want to try to avert or atone for God's extraordinary wrath by performing an extraordinary penance.

Most clerical observers were naturally hostile to the movement, since its members sometimes made extravagant claims for their flagellation, which potentially could obviate the need for the penitential sacrament. Blood shed from overenthusiastic whipping was compared to that which came from Christ as he hung on the cross, whose passion the flagellants claimed to be imitating. Popular belief also attributed to flagellant ceremonies the power to ward off the plague, or even to bring the dead back to life. But even when chroniclers derided the movement as a dangerous "sect," a skeptic like the Dominican, Heinrich of Herford, nevertheless testified to the exceptional emotion that flagellant ceremonies could arouse in spectators, to the point that "one would need a heart of stone to be able to watch this without tears."

The artistic impact of the Black Death is perhaps the hardest to pin down. By their very nature, art and literature lend themselves largely to subjective assessment, which measures their influences in patterns of long duration rather than immediate consequences. It is therefore probably a doomed exercise to attempt to draw a direct connection between plague and artistic productions. Nevertheless, some scholars, such as Millard Meiss, have argued for at least an indirect link, on the grounds that by the very act of killing off a generation of leading artists, the Black Death dealt a severe setback to the new humanism and inaugurated a less daring, more conservative style of expression. But since the subject matter of the art under consideration does not reference the plague at all, the connection remains ambiguous. More apropos is the *memento mori*, or "remembrance of death" art, that typically features a rotting cadaver or skeleton, thought to remind viewers of their own, impending death. Although this genre began well before the Black Death, its often apocalyptic and leveling message that all must die, no matter the social status or spiritual preparedness of the soul, seems to be especially in tune with the arbitrary mortality experienced during the plague. The usual interpretation of this macabre art, especially the Dance of Death motifs and transi tombs which depict the patron as a corpse, is that it is indicative of a society "obsessed" with decay and death. But an alternative view sees the cadaver or skeleton as a transitional figure, one that points instead to the resurrection and restoration of the body at the Last Judgment, when humankind would at last triumph over death. One can imagine that such a message also would have had great appeal during the Black Death.

That there was a "waning," or decline, of late medieval culture as a result of the plague and other crises remains a popular notion among students of the Middle Ages. But this fails to explain how this very same culture saw the stirrings of the dynamic Renaissance and humanism movements. The people of the later Middle Ages did not simply succumb to a "profound pessimism" associated with mass death. Instead, they possessed a confident outlook that put even an apocalyptic disaster of the magnitude of the Black Death into the perspective of God's secure and benevolent plan for humankind. The English anchoress and mystic Julian of Norwich, who lived through no less than eight major outbreaks of plague, including the one of 1348–1349, was yet able to declare in her "showings" that "alle shalle be wele" with the world. If chroniclers of the plague wrote as if the Apocalypse, the end of creation, was at hand, that event also signified in medieval eschatology that a new beginning would take the place of the decadent old. No longer can we afford to write off Europe at the end of the Middle Ages as a wasted society waiting for the modern era to begin. Rather, Europe's rebirth was forged in the crucible of its terrible yet transcendent ordeal with the Black Death.

SOURCES

The Societal Impact of the Black Death in Italy

The Florentine author Giovanni Boccaccio, an eyewitness to the plague's impact upon his native city, provides in his famous introduction to *The Decameron*, which is excerpted below, the classic depiction of what seem to be standard, perhaps universal, human responses to epidemic disease.

Another Italian humanist writer, Boccaccio's friend and contemporary Francesco Petrarch, while likewise dealing with the detrimental social effects that plague can have, also explored the profound question of how the disease affects the way generations view and respond to each other across historical time. In a letter written in May 1349 from Parma to his friend Louis Sanctus, at the papal court of Avignon, Petrarch pointedly questioned whether both past and future societies can even relate to his own when an event of the scale and magnitude as the Black Death happens to strike a hapless generation:

> When will posterity believe this to have been a time in which nearly the whole world – not just this or that part of the earth – is bereft of inhabitants, without there having occurred a conflagration in the heavens or on land, without wars or other visible disasters? When at any time has such a thing been seen or spoken of? Has what happened in these years ever been read about: empty houses, derelict cities, ruined estates, fields strewn with cadavers, a horrible and vast solitude encompassing the whole world? Consult historians, they are silent; ask physicians, they are stupefied; seek the answer from philosophers, they shrug their shoulders, furrow their brows, and with fingers pressed against their lips, bid you be silent. Will posterity believe these things, when we who have seen it can scarcely believe it, thinking it a dream except that we are awake and see these things with our open eyes, and when we know that what we bemoan is absolutely true, as in a city fully lit by the torches of its funerals we head for home, finding our longed-for security in its emptiness? O happy people of the next generation, who will not know these miseries and most probably will reckon our testimony as a fable![1]

Boccaccio and Petrarch were among the most prescient observers of the Black Death. For both authors, the unprecedented mortality of the disease stirred a newfound realization that a writer could be a subjective commentator on his times, rather than simply a recorder of a history already written by God's salvation plan for the human race. This in turn spurred both men to go beyond mere chronicling of an extraordinary historical event to assessing the social and psychological impact that the plague had upon their society's customs, mores, and outlook. In a sense, the plague forced these men to respond with their own, unique, individual observations rather than with the standard denunciations of moral laxity that is fairly typical of medieval chronicles. And this sort of individualism was, after all, to become a hallmark of the later Renaissance. The Black Death thus can be considered a liberator of late medieval written culture, freeing it from the shackles of age-old usage, and in this way may well have constituted a turning point in historical writing.[2]

■ Giovanni Boccaccio, Introduction to *The Decameron*, 1349–1351

A leading figure of the early Italian Renaissance, Giovanni Boccaccio (1313–1375) helped create the first vernacular literature in Italian. He was born in or near Florence, and his father intended him to have a banking career, but eventually Boccaccio devoted himself to writing literature. Although he spent the 1330s in Naples at the court of Robert of Anjou, Boccaccio came back to Florence in 1341 in time to witness the ravages of the Black Death, which he describes in the introduction to his most famous work, *The Decameron*, composed between 1349 and 1351. A perceptive observer of human psychology, it probably was no accident that he also wrote what many consider to be the first psychological novel, *The Elegy for Lady Fiammetta*, but a few years before the arrival of the Black Death. Boccaccio was more interested in plumbing the psychic and social consequences of the plague than in describing its physical or clinical aspects.

It has been said that the Black Death severed, at least temporarily, many of the bonds and norms that held medieval society together. As you read Boccaccio's description of the plague's course and consequences, try to identify those severed bonds and norms. More than that, also try to assess the level of credence that you can give to Boccaccio's description. Do his words ring true, or are we dealing with misleading stereotypes, fanciful literary tropes, or gross exaggerations?

Source: Giovanni Boccaccio, *The Decameron*, trans. G.H. McWilliam (Harmondsworth, Middlesex: Penguin Books, 1972), 51–56.

It is a remarkable story that I have to relate. And were it not for the fact that I am one of many people who saw it with their own eyes, I would scarcely dare to believe it, let alone commit it to paper, even though I had heard it from a person whose word I could trust. The plague I have been describing was of so contagious a nature that very often it visibly did more than simply pass from one person to another. In other words, whenever an animal other than a human being touched anything belonging to a person who had been stricken or exterminated by the disease, it not only caught the sickness, but died from it almost at once. To all of this, as I have just said, my own eyes bore witness on more than one occasion. . . .

These things, and many others of a similar or even worse nature, caused various fears and fantasies to take root in the minds of those who were still alive and well. And almost without exception, they took a single and very inhuman precaution, namely to avoid or run away from the sick and their belongings, by which means they all thought that their own health would be preserved.

Some people were of the opinion that a sober and abstemious mode of living considerably reduced the risk of infection. They therefore formed themselves into groups and lived in isolation from everyone else. Having withdrawn to a comfortable abode where there were no sick persons, they locked themselves in and settled down to a peaceable existence, consuming modest quantities of delicate foods and precious wines and avoiding all excesses. They refrained from speaking to outsiders, refused to receive news of the dead or the sick, and entertained themselves with music and whatever other amusements they were able to devise.

Others took the opposite view, and maintained that an infallible way of warding off this appalling evil was to drink heavily, enjoy life to the full, go round singing and merrymaking, gratify all of one's cravings whenever the opportunity offered, and shrug the whole thing off as one enormous joke. Moreover, they practiced what they preached to the best of their ability, for they would visit one tavern after another, drinking all day and night to immoderate excess; or alternatively (and this was their more frequent custom), they would do their drinking in various private houses, but only in the ones where the conversation was restricted to subjects that were pleasant and entertaining. Such places were easy to find, for people behaved as though their days were numbered, and treated their belongings and their own persons with equal abandon. Hence most houses had become common property, and any passing stranger could make himself at home as naturally as though he were the rightful owner. But for all their riotous manner of living, these people always took good care to avoid any contact with the sick.

In the face of so much affliction and misery, all respect for the laws of God and man had virtually broken down and been extinguished in our city [of Florence]. For like everybody else, those ministers and executors of the laws who were not either dead or ill were left with so few subordinates that they were unable to discharge any of their duties. Hence everyone was free to behave as he pleased.

There were many other people who steered a middle course between the two already mentioned, neither restricting their diet to the same degree as the first group, nor indulging so freely as the second in drinking and other forms of wantonness, but simply doing no more than satisfy their appetite. Instead of incarcerating themselves, these people moved about freely, holding in their hands a posy of flowers or fragrant herbs, or one of a wide range of spices, which they applied at frequent intervals to their nostrils, thinking it an excellent idea to fortify the brain with smells of that particular sort; for the stench of dead bodies, sickness, and medicines seemed to fill and pollute the whole of the atmosphere.

Some people, pursuing what was possibly the safer alternative, callously maintained that there was no better or more efficacious remedy against a plague than to run away from it. Swayed by this argument, and sparing no thought for anyone but themselves, large numbers of men and women abandoned their city, their homes, their relatives, their estates and their belongings, and headed for the countryside, either in Florentine territory or, better still, abroad. It was as though they imagined that the wrath of God would not unleash this plague against men for their iniquities irrespective of where they happened to be, but would only be aroused against those who found themselves within the city walls; or possibly they assumed that the whole of the population would be exterminated and that the city's last hour had come.

Of the people who held these various opinions, not all of them died. Nor, however, did they all survive. On the contrary, many of each different persuasion fell ill here, there, and everywhere, and having themselves, when they were fit and well, set an example to those who were as yet unaffected, they languished away with virtually no one to nurse them. It was not merely a question of one citizen avoiding another, and of people almost invariably neglecting their neighbors and rarely or never visiting their relatives, addressing them only from a distance; this scourge had implanted so great a terror in the hearts of men and women that brothers abandoned brothers, uncles their nephews, sisters their brothers, and in many cases wives deserted their husbands. But even worse, and almost incredible, was the fact that fathers and mothers refused to nurse and assist their own children, as though they did not belong to them.

Hence the countless numbers of people who fell ill, both male and female, were entirely dependent upon either the charity of friends (who were few and far between) or the greed of servants, who remained in short supply despite the attraction of high wages out of all proportion to the services they performed. Furthermore, these latter were men and women of coarse intellect and the majority were unused to such duties, and they did little more than hand things to the invalid when asked to do so and watch over him when he was dying. And in performing this kind of service, they frequently lost their lives as well as their earnings.

As a result of this wholesale desertion of the sick by neighbors, relatives, and friends, and in view of the scarcity of servants, there grew up a practice almost never previously heard of, whereby when a woman fell ill, no matter how gracious or beautiful or gently bred she might be, she raised no objection to being attended by a male servant, whether he was young or not. Nor did she have any scruples about showing him every part of her body as freely as she would have displayed it to a woman, provided that the nature of her infirmity required her to do so; and this explains why those women who recovered were possibly less chaste in the period that followed.

Moreover a great many people died who would perhaps have survived had they received some assistance. And hence, what with the lack of appropriate means for tending the sick, and the virulence of the plague, the number of deaths reported in the city whether by day or night was so enormous that it astonished all who heard tell of it, to say nothing of the people who actually witnessed the carnage. And it was perhaps inevitable that among the citizens who survived there arose certain customs that were quite contrary to established tradition.

It had once been customary, as it is again nowadays, for the women relatives and neighbors of a dead man to assemble in his house in order to mourn in the company of the women who had been closest to him; moreover his kinsfolk would forgather in front of his house along with his neighbors and various other citizens, and there would be a contingent of priests, whose numbers varied according to the quality of the deceased; his body would be taken thence to the church in which he had wanted to be buried, being borne on the shoulders of his peers amidst the funeral pomp of candles and dirges. But as the ferocity of the plague began to mount, this practice all but disappeared entirely and was replaced by different customs. For not only did people die without having many women about them, but a great number departed this life without anyone at all to witness their going. Few indeed were those to whom the lamentations and bitter tears of their relatives were accorded; on the contrary, more often than not bereavement was the signal for laughter and witticisms and general jollification – the art of which the women, having for the most part suppressed their feminine concern for the salvation of the souls of the dead, had learned to perfection. Moreover it was rare for the bodies of the dead to be accompanied by more than ten or twelve neighbors to the church, nor were they borne on the shoulders of worthy and honest citizens, but by a kind of gravedigging fraternity, newly come into being and drawn from the lower orders of society. These people assumed the title of sexton, and demanded a fat fee for their services, which consisted in taking up the coffin and hauling it swiftly away, not to the church specified by the dead man in his will, but usually to the nearest at hand. They would be preceded by a group of four or six clerics, who between them carried one or two candles at most, and sometimes none at all. Nor did the priests go to the trouble of pronouncing solemn and lengthy funeral rites, but, with the aid of these so-called sextons, they hastily lowered the body into the nearest empty grave they could find. . . .

Whenever people died, their neighbors nearly always followed a single, set routine, prompted as much by their fear of being contaminated by the decaying corpse as by any charitable feelings they may have entertained toward the deceased. Either on their own, or with the assistance of bearers whenever these were to be had, they extracted the bodies of the dead from their houses and left them lying outside their front doors, where anyone going about the streets, especially in the early morning, could have observed countless numbers of them. Funeral biers would then be sent for, upon which the dead were taken away, though there were some who, for lack of biers, were carried off on plain boards. It was by no means rare for more than one of these biers to be seen with two or three bodies upon it at a time; on the contrary, many were seen to contain a husband and wife, two or three brothers and sisters, a father and son, or some other pair of close relatives. And times without number it happened that two priests would be on their way to bury someone, holding a cross before them, only to find that bearers carrying three or four additional biers would fall in behind them; so that whereas the priests had thought they had only one burial to attend to, they in fact had six or seven, and sometimes more. Even in these circumstances, however, there were no tears or candles or mourners to honor the dead; in fact, no more respect was accorded to dead people than would nowadays be shown toward dead goats. For it was quite apparent that the one thing which, in normal times, no wise man had ever learned to accept with patient resignation (even though it struck so seldom and unobtrusively), had now been brought home to the feeble-minded as well, but the scale of the calamity caused them to regard it with indifference.

Scapegoating and Jewish Pogroms during the Black Death in Germany

Scapegoating of minority groups seems to be an all too human failing in times of crisis, and medieval Christian society during the Black Death was no exception. The pogroms of 1348–1350 took place within the context of centuries of assaults and "blood libels" directed against the Jews by Christians. Jews were labeled as "Christ killers" and as Christendom's diabolical enemy by a tradition that held they had betrayed Jesus Christ to Pontius Pilate and had rejected him as the messiah. The first widely noted Jewish pogroms in Europe occurred in the immediate aftermath of the destruction of the church of the Holy Sepulcher in Jerusalem in 1009–1010; although this was done on the orders of the Egyptian caliph al-Hakim, the desecration of Christ's tomb was blamed upon Jews and provoked apocalyptic fears. During the First Crusade, a group of German crusaders led by Emicho, count of Leiningen, attacked several Jewish communities along the Rhine and Mosel in May 1096 with the intention of forcing baptism upon the inhabitants. Some Jews resisted and died at the hands of the crusaders; many others chose to avoid forced baptism by resorting to *kiddush ha-Shem*, a self-martyrdom that also involved the killing of loved ones to protect them from pollution at the hands of unbelievers. This act, which was intended as a sublime statement of faith in the One God, in the manner of Abraham's readiness to sacrifice his son Isaac (Genesis 22: 1–18), was re-enacted 250 years later during the Black Death by some Jews who immolated themselves in the face of persecutions occasioned by charges that they were murdering Christians. But two centuries before the Black Death, specifically in 1144, came the first recorded accusation of ritual murder against the Jews, when a community at Norwich, England, was charged with kidnaping and torturing to death a 12-year-old Christian boy, William, in mockery of the passion of Christ. It is hypothesized that this blood libel arose in the context of Christian doubts and uneasiness over the miracle of the mass, when the sacrifice of Christ's body and blood was said to be re-enacted on the altar. In the next century and a half, this and other libels, such as ritual crucifixion and cannibalism, sprouted in other towns in England, as well as in Germany, France, and Spain.

Once such outrages were believed, it was but a short step to accusing Jews of trying to kill *all* Christians. Nevertheless, there also was a long tradition going back to St. Augustine (354–430 C.E.), whereby the Church argued for a grudging toleration of Jews, since their conversion at the end of time would serve as witness to the final triumph of Christianity. Yet this tradition was beginning to be challenged by the thirteenth century, when it was believed that Jews had intentionally murdered Christ – knowing him to be the messiah – as opposed to acting out of ignorance, and it was widely expected that the Antichrist would be a Jew. In addition, the Fourth Lateran Council of 1215 mandated more rigid segregation of Jews from Christians, such as by the wearing of different clothing, which in most countries was imposed in the form of a yellow badge.

At the same time, the economic position of many Jewish communities in Europe was being steadily undermined. Since the eleventh century, Jews were increasingly barred from farming and other crafts and trades by Christian regulations and competition. The result was that by the middle of the twelfth century, they were being stereotyped as greedy moneylenders, practically the only profession left open to them because usury, or charging interest on loans, was technically off limits to Christians by canon law (the law of the Church). Yet during the thirteenth century, even the Jews' precarious position as moneylenders may have been under assault: In England, for example, oppressive taxation by an increasingly exploitative monarchy forced Jews to sell off their debt instruments to Christian lenders or else call in their loans, thus raising awareness and resentment of their unique economic role. With the expulsion of Jews from England in 1290 and from France beginning in 1306, a further concentration of Jews probably took place in the cities of Germany and Spain that still received them. Jews were becoming a dangerously exposed community surrounded by a hostile, and widely indebted, Christian one.

The specific accusation of well poisoning leveled against the Jews in 1348 was not unprecedented. In France and Spain, both Jews and Muslims were implicated in the so-called "Lepers' Plot" of 1321, which charged that Jews in collusion with Muslims had induced lepers to poison Christians. In France especially, this seems to have resulted in several local pogroms against Jewish populations and a kingdom-wide expulsion of the Jews in that year. It may be no accident that these were the same areas that saw the first attacks upon the Jews during the Black Death.

These attacks began in the spring of 1348, when pogroms against Jewish communities coincided with the arrival of the plague in Provence in southeastern France and Catalonia in northeastern Spain.

It is not exactly clear what precipitated these attacks, but accusations of well poisoning may have played a part, since medical authorities in these regions, such as Alfonso de Córdoba and Jacme d'Agramont, wrote plague treatises that endorsed the belief that enemies of Christianity could be responsible for the disease through poisoning of water, food, or air. Moreover, a letter dated April 17, 1348 from the municipal officials of Narbonne in Provence to their counterparts in Girona in Catalonia communicated the fact that poor men and beggars had confessed under torture to spreading the plague through poison, for which they were horribly executed. Although Jews were not directly implicated in the letter, it was ominously stated that others, vaguely identified as "enemies of the kingdom of France," had paid the culprits to do the deed. Yet there is no record of any accusation of well poisoning made against the Jews in these regions in 1348. According to a *takkanoth*, or communal petition, that was drafted at Barcelona in December 1354 by representatives of Jewish communities throughout Catalonia and Valencia, Christian mobs attacked Jews in time of plague out of a vague desire to avenge "the sins of Jacob". Although this may refer to the crime of well poisoning, it more likely relates to the Jews' status as unbelievers, toleration of whom was, in turn, one of the Christians' sinful behaviors for which God was supposedly chastising them with the plague.

The first open accusation of well poisoning leveled against Jews manifested itself in the autumn of 1348, when several Jews were tried for the offense at Chillon and Châtel in present-day Switzerland. Eventually, by February 1351, such accusations and executions were repeated in as many as 100 towns and cities, mostly in Germany, and encompassing thousands of victims. Even though these alleged offenses seem to have been treated as secular crimes, the preferred method of execution – burning at the stake – suggests the procedures of the Inquisition. Technically, Jews were exempt from the Inquisition, which concerned itself with investigating the faith of Christians, although temporizing Jewish converts to Christianity were subject to the Inquisition from the latter half of the thirteenth century. Moreover, the death penalty invariably inflicted upon Jews once they confessed would be a grave violation in a trial for heresy, where those who confessed and begged for mercy for at least the first offense received mercy. This leads one to ponder: If Jews had no hope of saving themselves, why did they confess? Torture, hope of saving family and friends, psychological coercion, all were possible motives. By the

FIGURE 1.2 Burning of Jews.   The burning of Jews in an early printed woodcut. Jews were a common scapegoat for the Black Death in medieval Germany.

same token, it is unquestionable that there was not a whit of truth to any of the accusations. Even a few Christian observers, such as Konrad of Megenberg, who authored our source selection below, saw through the ridiculousness of the charges, and he was joined by Heinrich of Herford and, above all, by Pope Clement VI, who in the bull *Sicut Judeis* continued a papal policy that stretched back to the twelfth century of seeking to protect Jews from attacks. Among other arguments, those who defended Jews pointed out that they were dying in equal numbers to Christians from the plague, and that many of the accusations seemed motivated by a greedy lust for the Jews's goods. Yet, sad to say, most contemporaries appear to have been thoroughly convinced that such a crime was perfectly possible and the Jews perfectly capable of committing it.

Perhaps the most intriguing debate concerning the Black Death pogroms is how closely these conform to the Holocaust perpetrated by the Nazis in the twentieth century. Some scholars believe there is not much connection, if at all. One historian working on a monumental history of the Holocaust argues that "anti-Judaism" during the Middle Ages was religiously based and therefore fundamentally different from modern, racial anti-Semitism.[3] He points out that medieval Christians did not always demand the death of Jews, but offered them the escape clause of baptism. Furthermore, some individuals, such as those mentioned above, spoke up in defense of the Jews during the Black Death. The town councillors of Cologne, as well as Pedro VI, king of Aragon, Albert II, duke of Austria, and Charles IV, king of Bohemia, also seemed willing, at least for a time, to try to protect their Jewish communities from the fury of the mob. Even so, much of this altruism toward the Jews was economically motivated, as were the attacks against them; this created a fascinating dynamic between city rulers, who were anxious to preserve the Jews as potential sources of tax revenue, and the populace, who were equally anxious to be rid of the debts they owed them.

Yet if we accept as a definition of anti-Semitism that Jews "are feared as symbols of subhumanity and hated for threatening characteristics they do not in fact possess," the connection between medieval and modern anti-Jewish sentiment becomes easier to draw.[4] Blood libels emerged, in this view, because medieval Christians needed an irrational foil to allay their quite rational doubts about their faith, and a similar atmosphere of uncertainty could be said to have existed in 1930s Europe. The methods of mass execution (within technological limits of the time) and justification of such horrors on the grounds that Jews constituted an international conspiracy are present in both cases. Indeed, the Nazis seem to have been well aware of such a connection and took full advantage of it: The May 1, 1934 issue of the Nazi newspaper *Der Stürmer* features a front-page article and illustration devoted to ritual murder, and the Nazi propaganda film *Der Ewige Jude* (*The Eternal Jew*) identifies Jews with rats, known by then to be carriers of the plague. Even if one cannot accept all the connections, the foreshadowings in the events of 1348–1350 of an even greater tragedy 600 years later are deeply disturbing.

■ Konrad of Megenberg, *Treatise concerning the Mortality in Germany,* 1350

Perhaps the most balanced and rational medieval author to comment on the pogroms against the Jews was the scientific writer, Konrad of Megenberg. In the following section from his *Tractatus de Mortalitate in Alamannia* (*Treatise concerning the Mortality in Germany*), he debates both sides of the question as to whether the Jews caused the plague through the poisoning of wells. Megenberg seems to have written this work in 1350.

As you read this document, try to understand Konrad's perspective and arguments. Was he a champion, or full-fledged defender, of the Jews, or was he something else? Understand that others, such as Pope Clement VI and Heinrich of Herford, offered the same arguments. If these arguments seem reasonable to you, why is it that so many others believed otherwise and acted accordingly?

Therefore it is commonly believed in Germany that certain men called the Jews, who declare themselves to be bound by the Mosaic law and practice circumcision and who deny the crucified Christ and the true God made flesh from a pure virgin for the sins of human kind, poisoned the water of wells used for drinking and other human uses with a very potent poison; and that they did so throughout the various regions of the world where Christians and men of other faiths live with them, chiefly in order that, once the people of the Christian religion are dead, the kingdom of the Jewish race and their status as the Lord's anointed may be restored, which was taken away from them by the word of God, that is, by the only begotten flesh of God. . . . And this belief is confirmed by the fact that in many wells and streams of Germany, little sacks have been found, which, so they say, are full of decay and brimming with the most deadly poison. This poison, so they affirm, was tested on brute animals, such as pigs, dogs, and chickens and other animals, by mixing it with something edible, namely bread or meat, so that in this way they would taste some of the vile poison. Immediately the animals succumbed to a most swift death and their life was snuffed out as in a moment.

And again, [they cite the fact] that very many men, commonly called "sack-bearers" or "sack-porters" [i.e., vagabonds], have been apprehended, who, when put to various kinds of tortures, confessed to this crime and did not deny it, namely that they brought this deadly matter [poison] to the crowded places of the world in order to kill all Christian men throughout the land. And what is surprising is how many of these "sack-porters" or poisoners were Christians, who, while in the midst of an all-consuming fire, swore with their last breath that they were

---

Source: Sabine Krüger, "Krise der Zeit als Ursache der Pest? Der Traktat De Mortalitate in Alamannia des Konrad von Megenberg," in *Festschrift für Hermann Heimpel zum 70. Geburtstag am 19. September 1971* (Göttingen: Vandenhoeck and Ruprecht, 1971), 866–868.

bribed by the Jews with money to commit this most wicked crime, that they were seduced into this evil by everything delectable in this world, nor could they restrain themselves in any way from their hearts' desire for these delights.

Therefore the Christian people throughout nearly the whole of Germany, moved by these reasons, rushed upon the Jewish race with fire and with a most violent fury stained their hands with their blood. And their nation perished, namely Hebrews of both sexes, at the hands of the Christians, so that neither the nursing infant nor the child enclosed in its mother's womb was spared. Oh, how much weeping and wailing and what fear of heart and hissing between teeth was to be seen among a forsaken people! You would have seen maidens and wives with an unforgettable look upon their angelic faces being slaughtered by stupid rustic men with axes and nailed clubs and other instruments of war without mercy, as if they were slaughtering pigs or strangling chickens that were destined for the kitchen. Also, sometimes in some places they [the Jews] shut themselves up in a house with the doors barred and, after setting the house on fire, they died by their own hands by slitting the throats of their children, along with their own. Oh, what a wicked and detestable crime [committed] by the parents, which is thus visited upon their children, so that justly "they say to the mountains: 'Come, cover us' and 'Blessed are the barren who have not given birth,' " concerning which He [Christ] spoke the truth to mothers when he was led miserably to be crucified for our sins: "Daughters of Jerusalem, weep not over me, but weep for yourselves and for your children." [Luke: 23: 28–30] For He knew what was to happen to them now and in times past.

But although the Jewish people are justly detested by us Christians in accordance with the fundamentals of the Catholic faith, which are proven not only by the words of the prophets, but are also confirmed by the most manifest miracles of God, which they [the Jews] stubbornly deny, nevertheless it does not seem to me that the said opinion concerning the cause of so general a mortality throughout the whole world, with all due respect to whomever is expressing it, can be totally and sufficiently maintained. My reasoning is as follows: It is well known that in most places where the Hebrew people had remained, they themselves had died in droves from the same exact cause of this common mortality, as in the city of Vienna in Austria and in the city of Ratisbon in Bavaria, as well as in castles and fortresses where they were concealed by certain Christian noblemen. But it is not likely that the same people who ardently desire to multiply themselves upon the land should with malice aforethought destroy themselves and others of the same faith. And again: After the wells and cisterns full of stagnant water have been purified, and even when the original source and complete origin of the gushing and flow has been secured and finally blocked off, the people, who never used other springs, [still] died in great numbers. To which one can also add that if there had been such poison that could infect brute animals, as our adversaries say they have tested on them, then without doubt horses, cows, and sheep and livestock that drink the water ought to have been infected and died in great number like humans, which has not been seen. Nor is it probable, as is claimed, that livestock get their water more often from rivers, so that thus they cannot be infected from such things as wells and trickling streams, since the whole populace of Bavaria [living] in the cities bordering on the Danube and other navigable rivers only use the water of these same rivers and most scrupulously avoid well water, and nevertheless they [too] have died.

Moreover, even after all the Jews in many places have been killed and completely driven out for nearly two years prior, the Death now first strikes these same places with a strong hand and powerfully conquers the men who remain there, as in the city of Nuremberg in Swabia and in the countryside roundabout. For this and similar reasons it does not seem to me that the pitiful Jewish race is the cause of this general mortality which has spread throughout almost the whole world. But with regard to popular opinion, the Jews say, in order to counter [their reputation] as "sack-porters," that the greed and hatred of the populace has dictated these things about them. Nonetheless, rumor, which all indulge in, is not completely worthless.

Religious Responses to the Black Death in Muslim Spain and Syria

Like Christianity, Islam formed its own set of responses to the plague, dating back to its very origins under the Prophet Muhammad (ca.570–ca.632 C.E.), whose career coincided with the continuation of the "Plague of Justinian" in the eastern Mediterranean. According to the Hadith, the collection of traditions compiled in the first centuries after Muhammad's death, the Prophet had forbidden flight from a plague-stricken area. Although less securely established by tradition, he also is alleged to have denied the concept of contagion, since God is the sole author of the plague, and to have welcomed plague as a mercy and martyrdom for the faithful and a punishment for the infidel. Submission to and death by plague thus became analogous to sacrifice in the Muslim holy war known as jihad: Both demanded courageous demonstrations of faith that were equally meritorious in God's eyes, and both were to be rewarded with immediate entry into paradise. The

Syrian author Ibn al-Wardi neatly summed up these attitudes when writing about the Black Death in Aleppo in 1348–1349 (see the first source selection below). It is claimed that Muslim attitudes toward plague constituted "a major theological invention" that was unique to Islam. Certainly, Islam and Christianity developed their own approaches to a theological explanation of plague, but there also was much that was similar in their religious responses to the Black Death.

Nonetheless, one can argue that there existed an insuperable gulf between medieval Christian and Muslim approaches to the plague. Christians showed little understanding or even awareness of the religious views of Muslims. The report of several European chroniclers that Islamic Mongols at the siege of Caffa in 1346 decided to convert to Christianity when afflicted by the disease is extremely unlikely. Even as well informed a chronicler as Matteo Villani of Florence displays his ignorance of Islamic culture when he declares that: "It commenced with the infidels [Muslims] this cruel inhumanity, that mothers and fathers abandoned their children, and children their fathers and mothers, one brother the other and other relatives, a thing cruel and astonishing, and something very foreign to human nature, detestable to faithful Christians, who yet soon followed the barbaric nations in practicing this same cruelty."[5] Given Islamic taboos against flight from a plague region, the exact opposite was more likely to be true.

There were, indeed, some fundamental differences in the way Islam and Christianity interpreted the advent and spread of the Black Death. Sunni Islam did not so readily draw upon its apocalyptic traditions as did Christians when it responded to the plague, and it is claimed that Muslims displayed no scapegoating tendencies against the Jews during the Black Death which were to become a notorious and tragic facet of the European experience (see above). In theory, Muslims viewed disease not as a divine chastisement for sin as in the Christian world, but as a natural disaster that God allowed with no reference to human culpability or punishment. Above all, Muslims rejected the concept of plague contagion, since this posed a cause of the disease outside the direct agency of God, whereas even the leader of Christendom, Pope Clement VI, bowed to this medical principle by fleeing from his plague-stricken seat at Avignon. The contrast is well illustrated by parallel stories told by Gilles li Muisis and Ibn Battuta: The Christian chronicler relates how some pilgrims "left in great haste" once they learned in the morning that their host and his whole family were dead; Ibn Battuta and his companion, on the other hand, stay to pray over and bury a faqir, or Muslim holy man, who died in their company during the night. Whereas Muslims continued to indulge in communal prayers, processions, and funerals even at the height of the plague, these were proscribed on health grounds by several Christian communities.

However, one should beware of making too much of this difference. Religious proscriptions against contagion do not seem to have interfered with the practice of medicine in the Muslim world, since this also was authorized by the Koran, and there seems to have been some debate within the Muslim religio-legal community, or *ulama*, concerning Islamic precepts on plague. One brave soul, the Moorish physician Ibn al-Khatib, who authored the second source selection below, openly subscribed to the theory of contagion on the basis of practical observation, even when his friend and colleague Ibn Khatima took the more prudent approach of only doing so tacitly. But the fact that Ibn al-Khatib was eventually lynched by a mob for his defiance of such long-held *fatwas* is proof that Muslims could be just as intolerant as Christians, even if they did not take it out on the Jews. Dispute between advocates of religion and science also could occur in the Christian community, as testified by Konrad of Megenberg, who reported hostile rivalries between religious and scientific theorists as to the cause of plague. Finally, in the thick of the plague, Muslims as well as Christians could seek to alleviate the disease through prayer, even though this conflicted with Islamic theology that it was a mercy and martyrdom. For both religions, of course, God was the ultimate author of the plague, and Christians as well as Muslims could be brought to admit that this terrible calamity could be a blessing in disguise that worked for the salvation of true believers, even if this was by the indirect means of inducement of reformed behavior. The Italian and Syrian chroniclers Gabriele de Mussis and Ibn Kathir tell almost identical stories of how prophecies uttered by holy men could spur renewed religious fervor among a populace threatened with plague. As always, animosity between the two religions hides much that they actually have in common.

■ Ibn al-Wardi, *Essay on the Report of the Pestilence,* ca.1348

Abu Hafs Umar ibn al-Wardi was born in Maarrat al-Numan, a town 60 miles south of Antioch in northern Palestine, in 1290–1292. After studying at Muslim schools in Hama, Damascus and Aleppo in Syria, he served as deputy to the *qadi,* or religious judge, of Aleppo until 1343, and thereafter devoted himself to writing. His collected works cover a range of topics, including grammar, history, law, mysticism, and the interpretation of dreams. Although plague came to the region, according to Ibn Battuta, in May or June 1348, it was not until March 18, 1349, that al-Wardi died of the Black Death in Aleppo, near his birthplace. His *Risala al-Naba' 'an al-Waba'* (*Essay on the Report of the Pestilence*) is therefore exactly contemporaneous with the disease. Using a style typical of Arabic scholastic writing, Wardi inserts poetic verses into the narrative to aid in memorization of the text.

As you read this text, compare its message with Boccaccio's description of how the plague was greeted in Florence (see above). How, according to the author, is the plague a sign of God's mercy and providential care for Muslims? Yet, why does he pray for its cessation? Why do you think Ibn al-Wardi wrote this passage?

This plague is for the Muslims a martyrdom and a reward, and for the disbelievers a punishment and a rebuke. When the Muslim endures misfortune, then patience is his worship. It has been established by our Prophet, God bless him and give him peace, that the plague-stricken are martyrs. This noble tradition is true and assures martyrdom. And this secret should be pleasing to the true believer. If someone says it causes infection and destruction, say: God creates and recreates. If the liar disputes the matter of infection and tries to find an explanation, I say that the Prophet, on him be peace, said: who infected the first? If we acknowledge the plague's devastation of the people, it is the will of the Chosen Doer. So it happened again and again.

I take refuge in God from the yoke of the plague. Its high explosion has burst into all countries and was an examiner of astonishing things. Its sudden attacks perplex the people. The plague chases the screaming without pity and does not accept a treasure for ransom. Its engine is far-reaching. The plague enters into the house and swears it will not leave except with all of its inhabitants: "I have an order from the *qadi* [religious judge] to arrest all those in the house." Among the benefits of

---

Source: Michael Dols, "Ibn al-Wardi's *Risalah al-Naba' 'an al-Waba,'* a Translation of a Major Source for the History of the Black Death in the Middle East" in *Near Eastern Numismatics, Iconography, Epigrapy and History: Studies in Honor of George C. Miles,* ed. Dickran K. Kouymjian (Beirut: American University of Beirut, 1974), 454–455. Reprinted by permission of the American University of Beirut.

this order is the removal of one's hopes and the improvement of his earthly works. It awakens men from their indifference for the provisioning of their final journey.

> One man begs another to take care of his children, and one says goodbye to his neighbors.
> A third perfects his works, and another prepares his shroud.
> A fifth is reconciled with his enemies, and another treats his friends with kindness.
> One is very generous; another makes friends with those who have betrayed him.
> Another man puts aside his property; one frees his servants.
> One man changes his character while another mends his ways.
> For this plague has captured all people and is about to send its ultimate destruction.
> There is no protection today from it other than His mercy, praise be to God.

Nothing prevented us from running away from the plague except our devotion to noble tradition. Come then, seek the aid of God Almighty for raising the plague, for He is the best helper. Oh God, we call You better than anyone did before. We call You to raise from us the pestilence and plague. We do not take refuge in its removal other than with You. We do not depend on our good health against the plague but on You. We seek Your protection, oh Lord of creation, from the blows of this stick. We ask for Your mercy which is wider than our sins even as they are the number of the sands and pebbles. We plead with You, by the most honored of the advocates, Muhammad, the Prophet of mercy, that You take away from us this distress. Protect us from the evil and the torture and preserve us. For You are our sole support; what a perfect trustee!

■ Lisan al-Din Ibn al-Khatib, *A Very Useful Inquiry into the Horrible Sickness*, 1349–1352

A Muslim scholar and physician, Lisan al-Din Ibn al-Khatib hailed from Loja, a town near Granada, the capital city of an important and tenacious Moorish kingdom in southern Spain. A friend of the famous plague doctor Ibn Khatima, Ibn al-Khatib wrote his own medical account of the plague, entitled *Muqni'at as-sa'il 'an al-marad al-ha'il* (*A Very Useful Inquiry into the Horrible Sickness*). It was probably composed between 1349 and 1352, since al-Khatib's account of

the plague incorporates that of his friend Ibn Battuta, who was visiting Granada at that time. In this excerpt, Ibn al-Khatib gives his
reasons for rejecting the Islamic religious prescription against the
theory of plague contagion, which was well attested by physicians.
His outspokenness against a long-established hadith, or religious
tradition, backed up by Sharia, or Islamic law, was perhaps
triggered by the fact that his friend Ibn Khatima felt compelled to
bow to Islamic precept over empirical observation on this same
subject in his own treatise. Ibn al-Khatib's brave defense of contagion perhaps contributed to his forced exile from Granada in 1371,
when proceedings were begun for his trial for heresy on the basis of
his writings. Before the trial could begin, however, a mob broke
into his prison at Fez and strangled him in 1374.

How does Ibn al-Khatib use both reason supported by empirical
observation and Islamic piety to argue for the theory of contagion?
Why does he use the latter and not just the former? Compare Ibn al-
Khatib's method of argumentation with that of Konrad of Megenberg
(see above). How are they similar, and how do they differ? Which is
more significant, and why?

If it were asked, how do we submit to the theory of contagion [of the
plague], when already the divine law has refuted the notion of contagion, we will answer: The existence of contagion has been proved
by experience, deduction, the senses, observation, and by unanimous reports, and these aforementioned categories are the demonstrations of proof. And it is not a secret to whoever has looked into
this matter or has come to be aware of it that those who come into
contact with [plague] patients mostly die, while those who do not
come into contact survive. Moreover, disease occurs in a household
or neighborhood because of the mere presence of a contagious dress
or utensil; even a [contaminated] earring has been known to kill
whoever wears it and his whole household. And when it happens in
a city, it starts in one house and then affects the visitors of the house,
then the neighbors, the relatives, and other visitors until it spreads
throughout the city. And coastal cities are free of the disease until it
comes from the sea through a visitor from another city that has the

---

Source: M.J. Müller, "Ibnulkhatib's Bericht über die Pest," *Sitzungsberichte der Königl. Bayerischen
Akademie der Wissenchaften*, 2 (1863): 2–12. Translated from the Arabic with assistance from
Dr. Walid Saleh.

disease, and thus the appearance of the disease in the safe city coincides with the arrival of this man from the contagious city. And the safety of those who have gone into isolation is demonstrated by the example of the ascetic,* Ibn Abu Madyan, who lived in the city of Salé [unidentified]. He believed in contagion, and so he hoarded food and bricked up the door on his family (and his family was large!), and the city was obliterated by the plague and not one soul [except Ibn Abu Madyan] was left in that whole town. And reports were unanimous that isolated places that have no roads to them and are not frequented by people have escaped unscathed from the plague. And let me tell you of the miraculous survival in our time of the Muslim prisoners who were spared [the plague] in the prison of the city of Seville,† and they were in the thousands. They were not struck by the bubonic plague, yet it almost obliterated the city. And it has been confirmed that nomads and tent dwellers in Africa and other nomadic places have escaped unscathed because their air is not enclosed and it is improbable that it can be corrupted.

And amidst the horrible afflictions that the plague has imposed upon the people, God has afflicted the people with some learned religious scholars who issue *fatwas*‡ [against fleeing the plague], so that the quills with which the scholars wrote these *fatwas* were like swords upon which the Muslims died . . . Although the intent of the divine law is innocent of harm, when a prophetic statement is contradicted by the senses and observation, it is incumbent upon us to interpret it in a way so that the *hadith* fits reality, even if we claim to subscribe to the literal meaning of the *hadith* and, lest we forget, to the fundamentals of the *Sharia* that everybody knows about. And the truth of this matter is that it should be interpreted in accordance with those who affirm the theory of contagion. Moreover, there are in the divine law many indications that support the theory of contagion, such as the statement of Muhammad: "A disease should not visit a healthy man," or the statement that: "One escapes the fate of God to meet the fate of God." But this is not the place to go on at length concerning this matter, because the discussion about whether the divine law agrees or disagrees with the contagion theory is not the business of the medical art, but is incidental to it. And in conclusion, to ignore the proofs for plague contagion is an indecency and an affront to God and holds cheap the

---

*A holy man who lives a life of extreme self-denial.
†Muslim warriors and others held captive by Spanish Christians.
‡A *fatwa* is a ruling or opinion based on Islamic law handed down by a qualified legal scholar; *fatwas* continue to be issued and observed in much of the Arab world to this day.

lives of Muslims. And some of the learned holy men have retracted their *fatwas* for fear of helping people to their deaths.

May God keep us from committing error in word and deed!

NOTES

1. Francesco Petrarch, *Epistolae de Rebus Familiaribus et Variae*, ed. Giuseppe Fracassetti, 3 vols. (Florence: Typis Felicis Le Monnier, 1859–1863), 1: 438–440.

2. Timothy Kircher, "Anxiety and Freedom in Boccaccio's History of the Plague of 1348," *Letteratura Italiana Antica* 3 (2002): 319–357.

3. S.T. Katz, *The Holocaust in Historical Context, Volume 1: The Holocaust and Mass Death before the Modern Age* (Oxford: Oxford University Press, 1994).

4. Gavin Langmuir, *Toward a Definition of Antisemitism* (Berkeley and Los Angeles: University of California Press, 1990), 301–302. For criticisms of Langmuir's definition of anti-Semitism, see Robert Chazan, *Medieval Stereotypes and Modern Antisemitism* (Berkeley and Los Angeles: University of California Press, 1997), 127–134. Chazan rejects the use of both terms, anti-Judaism and anti-Semitism, as applied to medieval anti-Jewish behavior.

5. Matteo Villani, *Cronica,* ed. Giuseppe Porta, 2 vols. (Parma: Fondazione Pietro Bembo, 1995), 1: 12.

American Holocaust: Smallpox in the Americas, 1518–1670

THE DEMOGRAPHIC IMPACT OF NEW DISEASES IN THE AMERICAS

There is, perhaps, no more controversial subject in the scholarly world today than the role and impact of disease upon the indigenous history of the American continent. Native Americans were by no means disease-free prior to the arrival of Christopher Columbus in 1492. Like every other civilization, they suffered from a variety of gastrointestinal, respiratory, and venereal infections. Nevertheless, there is no disputing the fact that closely attending the European colonization of Central, South, and North America, as well as the Caribbean, an un-heralded "hurricane" of virulent and variegated illnesses descended upon the natives, for whom there had been no prior exposure, and therefore virtually no immunological defense. And among the most deadly of these so-called "virgin-soil" epidemics was smallpox.

SMALLPOX: ITS EARLY HISTORY AND MANIFESTATIONS

Smallpox may be one of the oldest diseases known to humans. Although it is unlikely to have been able to sustain epidemics among prehistoric populations of nomadic hunter-gatherer societies, it probably established itself with the first civilizations of ancient Mesopotamia and Egypt. Smallpox seems to be described in Hindu texts from ancient India as early as 1500 B.C.E., and it has left traces that are still to be seen on the Egyptian mummy of Pharaoh Ramses V, who died in 1157 B.C.E. Smallpox may have been the disease described by the historian Thucydides during the "Plague of Athens" of 430–426 B.C.E. and by the physician Galen during the "Plague of Antoninus" in the Roman Empire during the second century C.E. It also may have struck China and Japan during the fourth and eighth centuries C.E. Smallpox was first positively identified by the Arab physician Rhazes, who distinguished it from measles in his *Treatise on Smallpox and Measles,* written in the ninth century in Baghdad. Already smallpox had the reputation as a childhood disease, which indicates that it was quite common and endemic throughout the Middle Ages.

Smallpox got its name toward the end of the fifteenth century, when the disease known simply as the "pox" became "small" to distinguish its pustules from the "greater" pox of syphilis, a venereal disease which may have been re-introduced to Europe in a new, more virulent strain from the Americas. Caused by a virus, smallpox occurred in two forms: *variola major,* which killed at a rate of typically 25–30 percent and played the greater role in history, and *variola minor,* which only had a 1 percent death rate but still conferred lasting immunity to its more lethal cousin. Once in the body, the virus incubated for a period of 9–12 days, after which the victim experienced violent fever accompanied by chills, nausea, aches and pains, and sometimes convulsions and delirium. If no internal hemorrhaging occurred, as happened in cases of "fulminating" smallpox, the victim lived on for another 2–5 days before the characteristic rash and pustules appeared, beginning on the face and then spreading to other parts of the body. If the pustules overlapped and completely covered the skin, a condition known as "confluent" smallpox, this usually heralded death as the body's natural defense against secondary, bacterial infections broke down; otherwise, the pustules, fewer and more widely spaced, eventually dried up into scabs and fell off, leaving the telltale "pockmarks" on the victim's face. Smallpox was easily communicated from person to person through droplet or breath infection, but the virus also lived on in the patient's pus and scabs, even after death, which likewise could be ingested by the next victim.

DEFENSES AGAINST SMALLPOX

No cure has ever been found for smallpox, but for survivors of both forms of the disease, there was the comfort of knowing they would never have to experience its ravages again. Hence some had themselves deliberately infected with the virus, usually through introducing a tiny amount of smallpox "matter" into an incision made in the skin, a practice known as "variolation," from *variola*, the Latin word for pustule. (In China, variolation took the form of inhaling old dried-up scabs, a practice apparently dating to the eleventh century.) Usually, the infectious pus or scabs used in variolation were taken from mild cases of the disease and rarely resulted in death. The epidermal method of variolation was introduced by the early eighteenth century into Europe and America, from much older traditions practiced in Africa and Turkey. But in 1796, an even safer alternative was introduced to the world by Dr. Edward Jenner of Gloucestershire, who inoculated an eight-year-old boy, James Phipps, with cowpox virus, which conferred immunity to its human cousin but without the dreaded symptoms. Jenner, however, was not the first to invent this technique, known as "vaccination," from the Latin word, *vacca*, for cow. It was known, for example, decades earlier in some parts of the English countryside where milkmaids suffered little from smallpox, and vaccination was apparently practiced since ancient times in India.

Vaccination became an emblem of not only protection against smallpox, but as a technique that could work on other viral infections as well, such as influenza. It also represented the possibility of completely eradicating disease. A global campaign to eliminate smallpox, begun in 1966, achieved its desired result in South America by 1972, in Asia by 1975, and in Africa by 1977. After two years went by with no known outbreaks of the disease, the Global Commission for the Eradication of Smallpox, sponsored by the World Health Organization, declared the official end of smallpox in 1979. Yet the virus lives on, in supposedly secure laboratories at the Centers for Disease Control in Atlanta and at the Russian Research Institute for Viral Preparations in Koltsovo. Controversy persists as to whether to destroy these last remaining stocks of the virus, first scheduled for execution in 1999 but since delayed, or to preserve and even replicate the surviving samples for research purposes, despite the fear that smallpox could revive through bioterrorism, should these samples fall into the wrong hands.

THE ARRIVAL OF SMALLPOX IN THE AMERICAS

Smallpox first landed in the New World in 1518 on the island of Hispaniola (modern-day Dominican Republic and Haiti). Its impact upon the native Taino population is famously described by the Dominican friar Bartolomé de Las Casas, who arrived back on the island in 1520:

> A terrible plague came, and almost everyone died, very few remained alive. This was smallpox, which was given to the miserable Indians by some person from Castile; the feverish Indians, who were accustomed, when they could, to bathing in the rivers, threw themselves in anguish into the water, sealing the illness into their bodies, and so, as it is a destructive disease, they die in a short time . . . I do not believe that 1,000 souls escaped this misery, from the immensity of people that lived on this island and which we have seen with our own eyes.

While some scholars claim that Las Casas exaggerated the mortality from smallpox on Hispaniola, other contemporary observers estimated that between one-third to one-half of the island's population died in the epidemic.[1] This does not preclude the possibility that other diseases may have invaded the island prior to 1518, especially after the second voyage of Columbus in 1493, when he imported large numbers of his fellow Europeans as well as foreign plants and animals.

Evidence suggests that smallpox arrived on the Mexican mainland in the spring of 1520 in the wake of the expedition of Hernán Cortes (see the first source). Thereafter, the disease proceeded southward into the heartland of Central America, and finally reached the Inca Empire in the South American Andes by the middle of the decade, apparently in advance of the Europeans. Notable among the dead at this time were Cuitláhuac, successor to Montezuma as leader of the Aztec Empire, in 1520, and Huayna Capac, ruler of the Inca

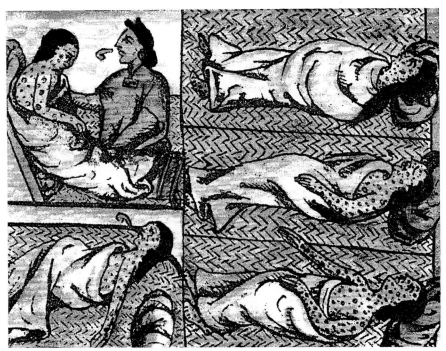

FIGURE 2.1 Smallpox Victims.   An illustration from the *Florentine Codex*, compiled by the Spanish Franciscan, Bernardino de Sahagen, ca.1585, which depicts the Mexica succumbing to smallpox during the epidemic of 1520 that coincided with Hernán Cortes' invasion and eventual conquest of the Aztec Empire. The illustration was probably drawn by a native picture-writer (see pp. 62–63).

Empire, in 1524. In both cases, their deaths created a leadership crisis that contributed significantly to the Spanish conquest. Smallpox continued to afflict Mexico, Central America, and the Andes during the 1530s, 1550s, 1570s, and 1580s. Other imported diseases that struck these regions throughout the sixteenth century included measles, mumps, bubonic and pneumonic plague, influenza, and typhus.

In North America, smallpox was also a leading killer of indigenous populations. Once again, smallpox may have raced ahead of European contacts, traveling up the Mississippi and Ohio River Valleys after being introduced in the Lower Mississippi region during the 1539–1542 expedition of Hernando De Soto. Cases of fulminating smallpox might have devastated natives in the American southwest during the 1580s and 1590s and in New England between 1616 and 1619, but we must wait until 1633–1634 before having definitive proof that the disease struck

MAP 2.1   European Colonization of the Americas.

the North American tribes. Some English colonists are recorded as having arrived in the company of smallpox at Boston in 1630, and shortly thereafter, the epidemic spread among the natives of Massachusetts and Connecticut. Indeed, this decade seems to have been a decisive turning point in the disease history of North America, for, according to one scholar, after 1640 "small pox was never absent" from the region.[2] It struck local communities of indigenous peoples in the northeast at least once a decade throughout the rest of the seventeenth century. In conjunction with other diseases, these epidemics are thought to be responsible for an astounding 75 percent reduction in the native population of New England by mid-century and perhaps almost total extinction by the century's end.

THE IMPACT OF NEW DISEASES UPON AMERICAN INDIANS

The popular perception that smallpox was the conquistadors' greatest weapon, spelling doom for the Native Americans in epidemics of "holocaust" proportions, has been central to the arguments of those who claim an overlarge role for disease in world history. But there certainly were other factors associated with European colonialism that contributed to native depopulation. War, slavery, abusive treatment, forced labor and migrations, and cultural imperialism, which possibly led to lower birth rates and even abortions and suicides, might all have taken their grim toll. Yet even in the sixteenth century some observers, such as Motolinía (the author of our first source), acknowledged disease as the natives' greatest enemy, and most modern historians have followed this lead. One scholar has gone so far as to declare "that it is virtually certain that epidemics were responsible for the bulk of Amerindian population decline in the sixteenth century. Since epidemics can account for virtually all of the extra mortality in the sixteenth century, the principle of Occam's razor [that the simplest explanation is best] suggests that it is not necessary to assume that there were other important causes of death . . . [T]he presumption of disease mortality as the overwhelming cause of Amerindian population decline throughout the New World seems virtually irrefutable."[3] Yet, quite recently one historian has called for a correction of the view that disease was the primary or sole cause of indigenous depopulation on three grounds: North America was by no means disease-free prior to 1492; native mortalities from smallpox and other "virgin-soil" epidemics were no different from the experiences of first exposure to disease in other parts of the world; and European violence and oppression impeded recovery from, if not actually contributed to, mortality episodes. While this does not mitigate the impact of disease upon the demographic history of the New World, it certainly forces disease to share the stage with other actors in, what is by all accounts, a profound tragedy for humankind.[4]

THE NATIVE POPULATIONS OF THE AMERICAS

Closely bound up with this debate are disputes over the actual numbers of natives who disappeared from the American landscape – from disease or any other cause – during the sixteenth and seventeenth centuries. The issue is a crucial one, for it can determine the scale and scope of disease's role in the early modern history of the Americas. As expected, estimates of population loss, both on a continental and on a regional level, and even of the size of the American population upon European contact in 1492, vary widely. The chasm between low and high "counters" can be explained by the varying data sources available, as well as the differing methods for evaluating and projecting the data. Nor can it be ruled out that ideological assumptions are made of a pre-contact Native American "Eden" that inevitably experienced a post-colonial fall.

Sources for determining the Americas' native populations on the eve of contact with Europeans and for the several centuries that followed include anecdotal estimates by contemporaries – both native and European; census-type records kept by both civil and ecclesiastical authorities – based on tribute payments, registers of births and deaths, baptisms, and conversions; archaeological and anthropological artifacts, which include dwellings, agricultural patterns, and skeletal remains; ecological evidence, such as the "carrying capacity" of the land that could support a given population; and known mortality rates of identifiable diseases. Each of these sources has an associated methodology to extract meaning from the numbers, and each method has its weaknesses as well as its strengths. But the stakes are high. If central Mexico, for example, is assumed to have had a native population in 1605 of 1 million, then the difference in estimates at Spanish contact in 1519 between a low of just over 3 million to a high of over 58 million means a population decline of 67 percent versus 98 percent. Likewise, if native population of the Andes was 600,000 in 1620, then the difference between a population in 1532 of 2 million versus one of 37 million translates into a decline of 70 percent as opposed to 98 percent.

EPIDEMICS: INTENTIONAL GENOCIDE OR UNINTENDED CONSEQUENCES?

Since even the low estimates of contact populations point to catastrophic declines in subsequent indigenous numbers, some additional questions remain. One is whether introduction of disease by Europeans was intentional or not, contributing to accusations of genocide leveled against the conquerors. Perhaps the most famous example is that of Jeffrey Amherst, commander of British forces in North America, who in 1763 authorized Colonel Henry Bouquet at Fort Pitt to use germ warfare, in the form of smallpox-laden blankets, against the Ottawa tribe who were rebelling under their leader, Pontiac, along the Ohio frontier. "You will do well to try to inoculate the Indians by means of blankets," Amherst wrote, "as well as to try every other method that can serve to extirpate this execrable race." Other documents confirm that this strategy was actually carried out, and that smallpox did indeed make its appearance by the end of the year. During the American Revolution, fears were raised that the British would use the strategy again against their former colonists. But although some British colonists, such as Increase and Cotton Mather, openly gloried in the decline of their native rivals for land, they invariably attributed this state of affairs to God's providence rather than their own design. Spanish and French colonists, on the other hand, are thought to have been more invested in the preservation of their indigenous populations, since these were integral to their economic and missionary activities.

THE IMPACT OF DISEASE ON NATIVE CULTURE

Another issue concerns the impact upon indigenous society and culture of heavy and sustained disease mortalities. While late medieval Europe emerged from a century and a half of perhaps equally devastating depopulation from the Black Death with a demographic and cultural recovery, even renewal, during the Renaissance, Native American numbers and way of life, it is argued, has never recovered to this day from its "contact shock" with European diseases. The fact that Europeans and Africans were relatively less susceptible to Old World illnesses such as smallpox, while natives died in large numbers, along with the passing of tribal elders who preserved the cultural memory of their people, led to widespread demoralization and loss of faith in native institutions, customs, and religious beliefs that only contributed to the decline with lower birth and replacement rates. Native despair at their lot is often summed up for modern observers by the following entry from the Mayan chronicle, *The Annals of the Cakchiquels*, concerning a smallpox epidemic that struck in the spring of 1521:

> Great was the stench of the dead. After our fathers and grandfathers succumbed, half of the people fled to the fields. The dogs and the vultures devoured the bodies. The mortality was terrible. Your grandfathers died, and with them died the son of the king and his brothers and kinsmen. So it was that we became orphans, oh, my sons! So we became when we were young. All of us were thus. We were born to die![5]

Recent research, while not essentially challenging this view, has refined it. A study of Jesuit records from the Spanish colony in northwestern Mexico reveals that the onslaught of European diseases, including smallpox, upon indigenous populations beginning in the sixteenth century did undermine native confidence and belief in their own healing rituals, as practiced by shamans, or *hechiceros*. This opened the way for Jesuit missionaries to baptize large numbers of natives, who petitioned for the rite, as a "cleansing of the soul" that would "provide a protection from or cure for disease." Jesuit caretakers of the sick enjoyed numerous advantages over their native counterparts, which included immunity from disease, continued attention to – rather than abandonment of – the physical needs of their patients, which often aided recovery, and a belief system that provided a ready explanation for illness as divine punishment for sinful or idolatrous behavior.

An even more recent study argues for a revival of the "Black Legend" – namely the genocidal impact of Spanish colonialism as manifested in war, slavery, and similar forms of aggression and oppression – as a significant factor in the steep decline of indigenous numbers, which previously had been dismissed by many scholars of

New Spain. Although, in this view, disease retains its primary role in causing the native "holocaust," the Black Legend may help explain why indigenous populations failed to recover from heavy mortality strikes from disease, in contrast to demographic resilience in the Old World. Despite the fact that Native Americans responded in a fashion similar to that of Europeans when confronted for the first time with a major epidemic – reacting with a mixture of "terror, confusion, and despair" – their debilitating experience with colonialism ensured that natives were not to reap the social and economic benefits that often followed sudden demographic decline, as had accrued, for example, in Europe in the aftermath of the Black Death. This, just as much as hopeless resignation and even loss of the will to live, doomed indigenous populations to demographic marginalization or, at worst, oblivion.

SOURCES

Disease and the Conquest of Mexico

According to our best evidence, smallpox arrived in Mexico in the spring of 1520 in the form of an African slave stricken with the disease who was brought over as part of the expedition of Pánfilo de Narváez, the man who was charged by the governor of Cuba, Diego Velázquez, to arrest Hernán Cortés. This, at least, is the story told by the Franciscan chronicler, Toribio de Benavente Motolinía, who was writing some twenty years after the event. Even though Motolinía's account is repeated by two other chroniclers, Bernal Díaz del Castillo, a soldier in Cortés's expedition, and Francisco López de Gómara, Cortés's secretary, modern scholars have cast doubt on the story. Suspicion rests on two grounds: that Motolinía is unclear about the date of smallpox's arrival in Mexico, since in his *Memoriales* he gives a different date altogether, 1521; and that Motolinía most likely had little knowledge of how smallpox really came to Mexico, since contemporaries did not associate smallpox with person-to-person contagion. As was natural for a friar, Motolinía approached smallpox from a biblical rather than a scientific point of view, being mainly concerned to draw an analogy with the ten plagues from the Book of Exodus. Likewise, Motolinía's claim that half the native population died from the disease is suspect, since this seems to be based more on the Book of Revelation than on an actual head count. Yet it is undoubtedly true that smallpox did come to Mexico shortly after it ravaged the nearby islands of Hispaniola and Cuba in 1518 and 1519.

There is also much controversy concerning the role that smallpox played in Cortés's subsequent conquest of Mexico. After Cortés defeated his rival, Narváez, in a pitched battle in late May 1520, he attempted to take over the Mexican capital, Tenochtitlán, but was driven out on the night of June 30, the so-called *Noche Triste*. He and his men recuperated among their native allies in Tlaxcala and then commenced a siege of Tenochtitlán in May 1521 using twelve brigantines, or specially-constructed warships. The city fell in August, after much destruction and house-to-house fighting. In the meantime, the inhabitants of the Mexican capital had suffered from the smallpox. This much we know from the *Florentine Codex* compiled by Bernardino de Sahagún, who, although he may have been influenced by his fellow Franciscan, Motolinía, based his account largely on native testimony. While the *Florentine Codex* provides a vivid and accurate depiction of the symptoms of smallpox, it is rather vague on the demographic impact of the disease, stating only that "many people died." Another chronicle from the native perspective, *The Book of Chilam Balam of Chumayel,* points to the advent of smallpox, along with the invaders who carried it, as a turning point in the history of the Yucatan:

> There was then no sickness; they had then no aching bones; they had then no high fever; they had then no smallpox; they had then no burning chest; they had then no abdominal pains; they had then no consumption; they had then no headache. At that time the course of humanity was orderly. The foreigners made it otherwise when they arrived here.[6]

But how, exactly, this disaster affected the history of the conquest is not made clear.

The conquistadors were a little more specific as to the assistance they received from smallpox in their campaigns. Díaz del Castillo reports that the disease helped Cortés sack the city of Texcoco, allied with Tenochtitlán, on December 31, 1520. Although the Spaniards prepared for an attack from the city, this did not materialize "because between the Mexicans and the Texcocans there were differences and factions, and in addition they had been weakened by smallpox, which had caused great suffering and was spreading over all the land." As a weapon, disease can cut two ways, however. In a letter to his emperor, Charles V, Cortés grieved over the loss of his close friend and ally, Maxixcatzin, ruler of Tlaxcala, who had died of smallpox in late 1520. But we do not know what role, if any, smallpox played in the climactic siege of Tenochtitlán. Díaz del Castillo famously describes the scene in the capital once the city fell after a siege of 93 days:

> Let me tell you about the dead bodies. I swear that all the houses on the lake were full of heads and corpses. I have read of the destruction of Jerusalem, but I cannot believe that the massacre was greater than that of Mexico, although I cannot say for certain. The streets, squares, houses, and courts were filled with bodies so that it was almost impossible to pass. Even Cortés was sick from the stink in his nostrils.[7]

But most of these victims seem to have died from war and starvation, not disease. (The Spaniards had blockaded the city during their siege.) In the very next paragraph, Díaz describes how "there has been no other generation of people in many years that has suffered so much from hunger and thirst and prolonged war as these," and war and famine are likewise given large roles in the conquest by Motolinía, who lists them as his second and third plagues on Mexico. The *Florentine Codex,* in fact, states that the Mexicans had recovered from smallpox before the final battle commenced. What is indisputable, though, is that smallpox, striking the natives again and again throughout the rest of the century, completed its siege of Mexico that it had begun in 1520–1521.

■ Toribio de Benavente Motolinía, *History of the Indians of New Spain*, 1536–1541

Toribio de Benavente was a Franciscan friar from Spain who arrived in Mexico in June 1524. He quickly adopted the name "Motolinía," from a Nahuatl word meaning "poor," when he and his companions were greeted by natives with this epithet upon their arrival in their thread-bare habits. Although Motolinía began and ended his more-than-40-year career in the New World at the Franciscan monastery in Mexico City, he traveled extensively throughout Mexico and, for a brief period, to Guatemala. In the course of his travels he came to know his native hosts intimately and sympathetically, a knowledge that became the basis for his *History of the Indians of New Spain,* which was written over a period of several years, from 1536 to 1541. While Motolinía, like his more famous Dominican colleague, Bartolomé de las Casas, championed the Native American cause against their brutal exploitation by the Spaniards, he eventually fell out with Las Casas over his overall attitude toward the conquest. For Motolinía, Spaniards proved capable of evolving into humane rulers, something that was never admitted by his rival. In the following excerpt, Motolinía describes the smallpox epidemic of 1520 as one of ten plagues that afflicted the native Mexicans, just as Egypt was stricken with ten plagues in the Book of Exodus, an analogy that Motolinía makes explicit in his *Memoriales.*

According to Motolinía, what secondary factors exacerbated the smallpox epidemic's mortality rate? Do they seem like reasonable factors? Why did Motolinía believe that the subsequent measles epidemic proved less lethal? What does this account suggest to you about the ability of both the Spaniards and the Native Americans to deal with these diseases?

Source: Toribio de Benavente Motolinía, Motolinía's History of the Indians of New Spain, trans. and ed. Elizabeth Andros Foster (Westport, CT: Greenwood Press, 1950), 38.

God struck and chastened with ten terrible plagues this land and all who dwelt in it, both natives and foreigners.

The first was a plague of smallpox, and it began in this manner. When Hernando Cortés was captain and governor, at the time that Captain Pánfilo de Narváez landed in this country, there was in one of his ships a negro* stricken with smallpox, a disease which had never been seen here. At this time New Spain was extremely full of people, and when the smallpox began to attack the Indians it became so great a pestilence among them throughout the land that in most provinces more than half the population died; in others the proportion was little less. For as the Indians did not know the remedy for the disease and were very much in the habit of bathing frequently, whether well or ill, and continued to do so even when suffering from smallpox, they died in heaps, like bedbugs. Many others died of starvation, because, as they were all taken sick at once, they could not care for each other, nor was there anyone to give them bread or anything else. In many places it happened that everyone in a house died, and, as it was impossible to bury the great number of dead, they pulled down the houses over them in order to check the stench that rose from the dead bodies so that their homes became their tombs. This disease was called by the Indians "the great leprosy" because the victims were so covered with pustules that they looked like lepers.† Even today one can see obvious evidences of it in some individuals who escaped death, for they were left covered with pockmarks.

Eleven years later there came a Spaniard who had measles, and from him the disease was communicated to the Indians; if great care had not been taken to prevent their bathing,‡ and to use other remedies, this would have been as terrible a plague and pestilence as the former. Even with all these precautions many died. They called this the year of the "little leprosy."

[Motolinía's other nine plagues include 2) "the great number of those who died in the conquest of New Spain, especially around Mexico"; 3) "a very great famine which came immediately after the taking of the city of Mexico"; 4) "the *calpixques* or overseers, and the negroes"; 5) "the great taxes and tributes that the Indians paid";

---

*Francisco de Eguía, a porter in Narváez's entourage who died in Cempoallan. This account of the arrival of smallpox in New Spain is repeated, with only slight variations, in the chronicles of Bernal Díaz del Castillo and of Francisco López de Gómara.

†At this point, in Motolinía's slightly longer account in his *Memoriales*, he adds: "and this sickness seemed to them [Indians] to symbolize all the tribulations and plagues that for all of them everywhere had to ensue."

‡Throughout the Middle Ages and into the early modern period, European Christians regarded bathing as leading to immorality and, from a medical point of view, liable to open the body's pores to disease-causing miasma.

6) "the gold mines . . . it would be impossible to count the number of Indians who have, up to the present day, died in these mines"; 7) "the building of the great city of Mexico"; 8) "the slaves whom the Spaniards made in order to put them to work in the mines"; 9) "the service of the mines, to which the heavily-laden Indians traveled sixty leagues or more to carry provisions"; and 10) "the divisions and factions which existed among the Spaniards in Mexico."]

■ Bernardino de Sahagún, *Florentine Codex: General History of the Things of New Spain,* 1585

Bernardino de Sahagún (ca.1499–ca.1590), a priest of the Franciscan order of friars, sailed for New Spain in 1529 and joined the convent at Tlalmanalco in Mexico, where he remained for much of his life. Sahagún was an avid student of Nahuatl, the language of the Mexica, or Aztecs, and became renowned for his fluency in it. This led him to compile *The General History of the Things of New Spain*, today known as the *Florentine Codex* because the earliest and best extant version of his bound manuscript, or codex, has resided in Florence, Italy, since 1589–1590. Sahagún apparently began his work of compiling pictorial, oral, and written accounts of Mexica culture and history in the 1540s but completed the *Florentine Codex* only in 1585 after an earlier version was confiscated by royal order in the 1570s. Divided into twelve books, this encyclopedia of Mexica culture records in parallel Nahuatl and Spanish prose, as well as through numerous pictures apparently drawn by native picture-writers, the story of the indigenous people of Mexico as told by them. As Sahagún writes in his prologue: "Those who helped me . . . were old chiefs, well versed in all things, . . . who also were present in the war when this city [of Mexico] was conquered." Despite this, the *Florentine Codex* probably reflects Mexica history and culture as interpreted through Sahagún's eyes and in a way not to offend Spanish Catholic sensibilities. The following excerpt is from the twelfth book of the *Codex*, which tells of the conquest of Mexico. The text is accompanied by an illustration of Mexican smallpox victims (see p. 51).

This description of the smallpox epidemic of 1520 is extraordinarily detailed. What specifically does it tell us about the nature,

Source: Bernardino de Sahagún, *Florentine Codex: General History of the Things of New Spain, Book 12: The Conquest of Mexico*, trans. Arthur J.O. Anderson and Charles E. Dibble, 2nd revised edn. (Santa Fe, NM: School of American Research, 14/13, 1975), 83.

course, and impact of the disease? Compare it with Motolinía's account. Do they complement, supplement, support, or contradict one another? What do you conclude from your answer?

Twenty-ninth Chapter, in which it is told how there came a plague, of which the natives died. Its name was smallpox. It was at the time that the Spaniards set forth from Mexico.

But before the Spaniards had risen against us, first there came to be prevalent a great sickness, a plague. It was in [the month of] Tepeilhuitl* that it originated, that there spread over the people a great destruction of men. Some it indeed covered [with pustules]; they were spread everywhere, on one's face, on one's head, on one's breast, etc. There was indeed perishing; many indeed died of it. No longer could they walk; they only lay in their abodes, in their beds. No longer could they move, no longer could they bestir themselves, no longer could they raise themselves, no longer could they stretch themselves out on their sides, no longer could they stretch themselves out face down, no longer could they stretch themselves out on their backs. And when they bestirred themselves, much did they cry out. There was much perishing. Like a covering, covering-like, were the pustules. Indeed many people died of them, and many just died of hunger. There was death from hunger; there was no one to take care of another; there was no one to attend to another.

And on some, each pustule was placed on them only far apart; they did not cause much suffering, neither did many die of them. And many people were harmed by them on their faces; their faces were roughened. Of some, the eyes were injured; they were blinded.

At this time this plague prevailed indeed sixty days – sixty day-signs – when it ended, when it diminished; when it was realized, when there was reviving, the plague was already going toward Chalco.† And many were crippled by it; however, they were not entirely crippled. It came to be prevalent in [the month of] Teotlelco,‡ and it went diminishing in [the month of] Panquetzaliztli.** At that time the Mexicans, the brave warriors, were able to recover from the pestilence.

---

*The "feast of the mountains" was celebrated in the Mexican calendar between October 11 and October 30.
†A subject city of the Mexica to the southeast of the capital of Tenochtitlán on the edge of Lake Texcoco.
‡The "arrival of the gods," whose feast in the Mexican calendar was celebrated between September 21 and October 10.
**The "raising of flags," whose feast was celebrated between November 20 and December 9.

Disease and the Colonization of New England

If smallpox aided the conquest of Mexico by the Spaniards in 1520–1521, it no less helped in the colonization of New England by English settlers during the early decades of the seventeenth century. Yet there was undoubtedly a different dynamic at work with the disease as it spread northward. Whereas Spanish colonists and missionaries lamented over and tried to limit smallpox's devastating impact, because the natives were an integral part of the *encomienda* plantation system and the religious orders' conversion efforts, English Puritans and Pilgrims, who for the most part neither tried to exploit nor evangelize the natives with whom they came in contact, seem to have simply wanted them out of the way. As the Reverend Cotton Mather, an influential Puritan theologian of Massachusetts Bay Colony, wrote toward the end of the seventeenth century: "had we done but half so much as the French Papists [Jesuits] have done, to proselyte the Indians of our east unto the christian faith, instead of being snares and traps unto us, and scourges in our sides, and thorns in our eyes, they would have been a wall unto us both by night and day." English colonists' main interest in the New World seemed to be in either trade or land settlement, for which they competed with the Dutch for the former and with the natives, and even each other, for the latter.

Following in the wake of the Jamestown settlement of Virginia in 1607, another colonial enterprise led by William Bradford and a group of English Puritan exiles in Holland landed 101 passengers of the *Mayflower* at Plymouth Rock in Massachusetts in 1620. In 1629 a second colony was founded at Salem, and in the following year a large group of settlers landed at Boston with seventeen ships bearing 1,000 men and women. Fleeing persecution as well as pursuing profit, the Puritan stream flowing out of England westward became a flood, as 4,000 colonists settled in New England by 1634, followed by a total of 20,000 in 1640. By the century's end, the tide of England's colonial population of 250,000 was beginning to swamp the receding one of Native Americans, who by this time had been reduced in the Northeast by at least three-quarters of their original numbers, to just under 150,000.

Smallpox followed, and perhaps even preceded, this wave of English immigration to North America. During 1616–1619 an epidemic spread among the natives from Maine to Massachusetts, which was vividly described by a colonial observer writing in 1622:

> They [the natives] died on heapes, as they lay in their houses; and the living, that were able to shift for themselves, would runne away and let them

dy, and let there Carkases ly above the ground without buriall. For in a place where many inhabited, there hath been but one left a live to tell what became of the rest; the livinge being (as it seemes) not able to bury the dead, they were left for Crowes, Kites and vermin to pray upon. And the bones and skulls upon the severall places of their habitations made such a spectacle after my comming into those partes, that, as I travailed in that Forrest nere the Massachussets, it seemed to mee a new found Golgatha.[8]

Whether this was smallpox is not exactly known, but without a doubt the disease struck the New England tribes in 1633–1634, when it was described by William Bradford, among others. In both the previous epidemic and in the current one, Bradford claimed a mortality of 95 percent for the tribes of the Connecticut Valley. While Bradford wrote sympathetically of the natives' plight, Increase Mather, the father of Cotton Mather and also an influential Puritan minister and theologian who wrote some decades later, gloried in it, claiming the tragedy as a cause of celebration for the English:

> About the same time [1631] the Indians began to be quarrelsome touching the bounds of the Land which they had sold to the English; but God ended the controversy by sending the small pox amongst the Indians at Saugust, who were before that time exceeding numerous; whole towns of them were swept away, in some of them not so much as one Soul escaping the destruction. There are some old Planters surviving to this day, who helped to bury the dead Indians, even whole familyes of them all dead at once. In one of the wigwams they found a poor infant sucking at the breast of the dead mother, all the other Indians being dead also.[9]

For colonists like Mather, smallpox – a disease that seemed to spare the English while decimating the natives – was a potent weapon in their campaign for settlement and expansion. The disease was to strike New England again in 1638–1640, and then from the 1660s throughout the rest of the century, when it combined with war to wreak havoc on the Native American population.

■ William Bradford, *History of Plymouth Plantation*, 1633–1634

William Bradford was born in Austerfield, Yorkshire, in 1590 and seemed destined to be a yeoman farmer, like his father. But in 1606 he joined a Puritan Congregational church at Scrooby and later moved to

Holland. In 1620 he sailed on the *Mayflower* and was one of the Pilgrim fathers who made the landing at Plymouth Rock on the coast of Massachusetts. In 1621 he was elected governor of Plymouth Colony, an office he held almost continuously until his death in 1657. Bradford began writing a *History* of the colony in 1630 and continued to add entries until the year 1650, when the work ends. As was perhaps typical of most Puritans, Bradford's narrative combines his religious concerns with his mercantile interests, in the latter case consisting primarily of trade in beaver pelts, which the colonists obtained from the natives and upon which the Pilgrims relied to pay their creditors. Competition with the Dutch for this trade is also evident from the following excerpt. But, of course, our main interest is the smallpox epidemic of 1634 that Bradford describes as afflicting probably the Narrangasett and Connecticut tribes who lived along the Connecticut River. Although a few Puritan passengers who arrived at Plymouth Colony in 1631 do describe themselves or their children as being sick with the smallpox during their voyage, the more immediate cause of the epidemic, according to Bradford, was the Dutch traders who attempted to set up shop with the natives during the winter of 1633–1634.

Bradford's striking descriptions of native symptoms and response to the disease should be compared to those for the Mexica during the previous decade, as recounted by Motolinía and Sahagún (see above). Compare also Bradford's description of the social consequences of the epidemic with Boccaccio's account of the plague in Florence (Chapter 1). What insights follow from these comparisons?

I am now to relate some strang and remarkable passages. Ther was a company of people [Native Americans] lived in the country, up above in the river of Conigtecut, a great way from their trading house [at Plymouth] ther, and were enimise to those Indeans which lived aboute them, and of whom they stood in some fear (being a stout people). About a thousand of them had inclosed them selves in a forte. . . . Three or four Dutch men went up in the begining of winter to live with them, to gett their trade, and prevent them for [from] bringing it to the English . . . but at spring to bring all downe to their place. But their enterprise failed, for it pleased God to visite these Indeans

Source: William Bradford, *Bradford's History of Plymouth Plantation, 1606–1646*, ed. William T. Davis (New York: Charles Scribner's Sons, 1908), 312–313.

with a great sicknes, and such a mortalitie that of a 1000, above 900 and a halfe of them dyed, and many of them did rott above ground for want of buriall, and the Dutch men allmost starved before they could gett away, for ise and snow. But about Feb. they got with much difficultie to their trading house [i.e., the English trading house at Plymouth]; whom they kindly releeved, being allmost spente with hunger and could. Being thus refreshed by them diverce days, they got to their owne place, and the Dutch were very thankfull for this kindnes.

This spring [of 1634], also, those Indeans that lived aboute their trading house there fell sick of the small poxe, and dyed most miserably; for a sorer disease cannot befall them; they fear it more then the plague; for usualy they that have this disease have them in abundance, and for wante of bedding and linning and other helps, they fall into a lamentable condition, as they lye on their hard matts, the poxe breaking and mattering, and runing one into another, their skin cleaving (by reason thereof) to the matts they lye on; when they turne them, a whole side will flea of at once, (as it were,) and they will be all of a gore blood, most fearfull to behold; and then being very sore, what with could and other distempers, they dye like rotten sheep. The condition of this people was so lamentable, and they fell downe so generally of this diseas, as they were (in the end) not able to help on another; no, not to make a fire, nor to fetch a litle water to drinke, nor any to burie the dead; but would strivie as long as they could, and when they could procure no other means to make fire, they would burne the woden trayes and dishes they ate their meate in, and their very bowes and arrowes; and some would crawle out on all foure to gett a litle water, and some times dye by the way, and not be able to gett in againe. But those of the English house, (though at first they were afraid of the infection,) yet seeing their woefull and sadd condition, and hearing their pitifull cries and lamentations, they had compastion of them, and dayly fetched them wood and water, and made them fires, gott them victualls whilst they lived, and buried them when they dyed. For very few of them escaped, notwithstanding they did what they could for them, to the haszard of them selvs. The cheefe Sachem him selfe now dyed, and allmost all his freinds and kinred. But by the marvelous goodnes and providens of God not one of the English was so much as sicke, or in the least measure tainted with this disease, though they dayly did these offices for them for many weks togeather. And this mercie which they shewed them was kindly taken, and thankfully acknowledged of all the Indeans that knew or heard of the same; and their masters here did much comend and reward them for the same.

Disease and the Colonization of New France

The colonization of New France began at Acadia in present-day northeastern Canada in 1604, but shifted westward to the St. Lawrence River valley with the foundation of Quebec by Samuel de Champlain in 1608. Jesuit missionaries quickly followed in the wake of fur traders, setting up their headquarters at Quebec in 1625. From the beginning, the French colonial experience in the New World was different from that of the English in Virginia and New England and that of the Spaniards in the Americas. Because the French colonists were few and widely scattered, they relied more on cooperation and diplomacy with their Native American allies, rather than on extermination and displacement as in the English colonies and on domination and subjection as in the Spanish holdings. This policy was no doubt dictated less by any altruistic motives the French settlers might have felt and more by practical necessity and a desire to promote lucrative trade and commerce, as well as French control and influence over the region. The Jesuit missions among the Montagnais, Algonquin, Huron, and Iroquois tribes along the St. Lawrence and Great Lakes greatly facilitated the French colonial process. Although missionaries certainly knew and understood native culture perhaps better than anyone through constant living among their prospective converts, they were nonetheless inveterate promoters of the Catholic Christian cause and even attempted resettlement of native populations along the lines of Spanish *reducciónes*, a term that implied the natives were "reduced" from a "proud and untamed independence to a proper obedience to God's laws." In the end, however, Native American subjects of New France were accorded far more independence and autonomy than probably anywhere else in the New World.

From the very beginning, the French Jesuits' missionary efforts in New France were plagued by disease. Already in 1616, the *Jesuit Relations* (see below) tell of how the Micmac tribe of Nova Scotia associated the invaders with an epidemic of perhaps pleurisy and dysentery that broke out during 1611–1613:

> They [the natives] are astonished and often complain that, since the French mingle and carry on trade with them, they are dying fast and the population is thinning out. For they assert that, before this association and intercourse, all their countries were very populous and they tell how one by one the different coasts, according as they have begun to traffic with us, have been more reduced by disease. . . . Thereupon

they often puzzle their brains, and sometimes think that the French poison them, which is not true.[10]

Ironically, the fact that the Jesuits lived in close proximity with their charges and lavished spiritual and medicinal care upon them only increased native suspicions that the French were the cause of their illnesses, as indeed they unwittingly were, although trading contact with other Native American tribes also facilitated contagion. Although the Jesuits attempted to administer the best in up-to-date European medical treatment to the Indian sick, native healing practices, consisting of natural medicines as well as shamanistic rituals, seem to have held their own during these crises, judging from the Jesuits' complaints of their converts' backsliding. The Jesuits' attempts to convert and minister to the medical needs of the Native Americans were not helped by the fact that the natives were fearful of European technology, and they tended to regard the wandering Jesuits, or "Black Robes" as they were known, as sorcerers and witches. Nor did the Jesuits help themselves by insisting on baptizing the sick in their last hours and urging total conversion from native shamanistic practices as the price of salvation. In a chilling *Relation* from 1637, when an influenza epidemic raged through some Huron villages, Father François Le Mercier, who himself came down with the disease, reported growing hostility among the natives to the Jesuit presence. Rumors spread that the Black Robes induced death through their baptisms and images and that they even sacrificed "a little child in the woods by stabbing it with a bodkin, which had caused the death of a great many children." Anything the Jesuits did, even reciting their litanies, was interpreted as black magic, and more and more doors were closed to them, to the point that they could no longer visit villages. Eventually a general council was held by the Hurons to decide what to do with the Black Robes, and they narrowly escaped exile and death.

When smallpox invaded the Huron lands in late summer 1639, Father Jérôme Lalemant reported a new round of persecutions and accusations. Even though the disease most likely spread to the St. Lawrence valley through native visitors from New England, where smallpox had prevailed a few years earlier, the Hurons quickly made the connection between the foreigners and their misfortunes. "They observed," writes Lalemant, "with some basis in reason, that since our arrival in these lands, those who were nearest to us happened to be those most ruined by the diseases and that the towns that welcomed us now appear utterly exterminated." In a passage of surprising sympathy with native fears, Lalemant goes on to describe how Jesuit behavior and immunity only exacerbated the situation:

> At the same time, this false imagination seemed to be powerfully confirmed by the fact that they saw us going through the country using every means possible to gain access to the cabins and taking unheard-of pains to instruct and baptize the most seriously ill. No doubt, they said, we must have a secret understanding with the disease (for they believe that it is a demon), since we alone were all full of life and health, though we constantly breathed nothing but a totally infected air, staying whole days close by the side of the most foul-smelling patients, for whom everyone felt horror. No doubt we carried misery with us, since, wherever we set foot, either death or disease followed us.
>
> In consequence of all these sayings, many held us in abomination. They expelled us from their cabins and did not allow us to approach their sick, especially the children, not even to lay eyes on them. In a word, we were dreaded as the greatest sorcerers on earth.
>
> Wherein truly it must be acknowledged that these poor people are in some sense excusable. For it has happened very often, and has been remarked more than a hundred times, that where we were most welcome and baptized the greatest number of people was in fact where the greatest number died. Conversely, in the cabins to which we were denied entrance, though they were sometimes extremely sick, at the end of a few days one saw every person happily cured. We shall see in heaven the secret, but ever adorable, judgments of God herein.[11]

While the Jesuits may have held both a cultural and biological advantage in responding to Old World diseases such as smallpox, this proved to be a confounding two-edged sword in their efforts at religious colonization.

After the middle of the seventeenth century, with the effective extermination of the Hurons by both epidemic disease and attacks by their Iroquois rivals to the south, the Jesuits shifted their focus to converting the Iroquois and the remaining Algonquin and Montagnais tribes. This seems to have been accomplished during the 1660s and 1670s, when the Jesuits benefitted from direct intervention by the French crown in New France. At the same time, smallpox continued to pose a challenge to the Jesuits' efforts, striking the Iroquois population in 1662–1663, and the Algonquins in 1669–1670. But as the *Relation* of

Father Charles Albanel from the latter period testifies, the Jesuits by this time had a new and different dynamic with their native converts (see source selection below).

■ Charles Albanel, *Jesuit Relation of 1669–1670*

The Order of the Society of Jesus, better known as the Jesuits, began publishing in 1632 annual reports, which they called *Relations*, on the activities of their missionaries to convert the "pagan savages" of French Canada and continued until 1673. Printed in Paris in French, the *Jesuit Relations* were designed to communicate to readers back home the progress of colonization and missionary work, as well news of important events occurring among the Indian tribes of New France and descriptions of their customs, habits, and culture. Typically, the *Relations* consist of letters from priests out in the field, which would be sent to their superior at Quebec and then to Jesuit headquarters in Paris, both of whom would edit the accounts before sending them to the printer. Although the *Relations* clearly give an account of the Indians from the Western colonial point of view, they sometimes describe native "diabolical" practices – albeit in hostile terms – and even allow natives to speak in their own voice, as transcribed by the priest. In a time when literacy was not prevalent, either among natives or colonials, the *Jesuit Relations* supply a valuable resource, not least because their authors lived for years among the natives in their villages, learned their language, and observed and described their culture, even if they did not fully understand or approve of it. The following *Relation* consists of extracts from two letters written by Father Charles Albanel, who was sent to the Jesuit mission of St. Croix among the Montagnais and Algonquin tribes at Tadoussac in 1669.

As you read Father Albanel's accounts, continue the comparative analysis you began with the earlier documents in this chapter. How do Albanel's descriptions of native symptoms and response to the disease compare to those recounted by Motolinía, Sahagún, and Bradford? Compare also his description of the social consequences of the epidemic with that of Bradford. What insights follow from these comparisons?

Source: *The Jesuit Relations and Allied Documents*, ed. Reuben G. Thwaites, 73 vols. (Cleveland: Burrows Brothers, 1896–1900), 53: 59–61, 69–75, 79–81.

Nothing has given me keener sorrow than the sight of the incredible miseries and the destitution to which our poor Savages were reduced; and I have been obliged to dwell with them without being able to succor them in such unusual extremities. I confess to you that my heart was so keenly touched by this that I put that pain in the number of the severest I have ever experienced.

The smallpox, which makes as great ravages among these peoples as the plague, and the extremes of hunger and cold have been the principal evils that have afflicted this miserable colony; they have swept away from it about two hundred and fifty persons, both Montagnais and Algonquins, Papinachois and Gaspesiens [Micmacs], from the Mission of Sillery and from Tadoussac. . . .

On the 28th day of November [1669], the French Shallop* which had brought me hither arrived, loaded with fifteen or twenty sick persons. They all resembled Monsters rather than human beings, their bodies were so hideous, emaciated, and full of corruption. To me they were objects of compassion, and at the same time called for an exercise of charity. I tried to render them all the services in my power. . . .

On the fifth day of the same month, some Frenchmen went down to Isle Verte, which is not far distant from Tadoussac, and is formed in our great River Saint Lawrence. They found a Cabin full of dying persons, and came to beg that I would go and render them all the assistance I could. I had much difficulty in quitting my post, because the place where I was might have passed for a Hospital for the sick, and my presence there was every moment necessary.

Nevertheless, on the tenth day of December I resolved to go and visit those poor people who were dying on that Island, which was destitute of all aid, to comfort them, and administer to them the Sacraments of the Church. I carried them some provisions; and when, during the journey, one of our Sailors, loaded with Indian corn, broke through the ice, he was saved by a kind of miracle – God having regard, without doubt, to his charity toward the poor Savages.

On the eleventh day, I arrived at that Island, and saw there only living skeletons and bodies all disfigured, for they had already passed four whole days without having anything to eat. I began my duties with prayer, and, toward evening, prepared some Theriac,[†] of which I gave them some doses. It is a sovereign remedy against

---

*A boat.
[†]A theriac was a compound of elements usually mixed in a treacly syrup that was thought to neutralize the disease poison inside the body.

that kind of disease. On the following day, all made confession; and I gave holy Communion to those who were in a fit condition to receive it. . . .

And, as it is unjust to deprive our Frenchmen of the glory which they deserve in this connection, I will say to Your Reverence that they rendered me efficient assistance by the assiduous attentions which they bestowed upon our sick Savages, and upon their own comrades when there was need, in attending them, dressing their sores during their illness, and burying them after their death, without suffering the intolerable stench which came from those corpses to hinder them from rendering toward them the duties of a truly Christian charity. So far was this carried that I have even seen some of them, with an admirable courage and zeal, load the dead bodies upon boats in the icy waters; and then, unloading them, carry them on their shoulders, although the putrid matter ran from all parts upon their garments and cloaks. These noble acts of courage ought to raise a blush at their own effeminacy in an infinite number of Christians who have a horror of even hearing about what these men did not have a horror of doing.

That employment, severe and disagreeable though it was, did not fail to have its own delights and unction. It made me consider with pleasure that so many melancholy objects, so many tears, so many labors, and so much wretchedness at last find a happy issue in a death precious in God's sight, who crowns all a Missionary's sufferings, if he knows how to make a good use of them. And I was not a little consoled when I thought that, if our Church Militant suffered great losses this year, I had every reason to believe that the Church Triumphant had profited thereby.*

Moreover, it has been noted that God, choosing to reward our Frenchmen for the charitable assistance that they had given those poor Savages, preserved them as by a miracle. So true is this that, excepting one of their number who was ill, but quite lightly, none of them have experienced any injury.

I was the last to suffer any ill effects, having my whole head extremely swollen, and my face covered with pustules like those of smallpox. A severe earache came upon me, together with a furious toothache. My lips became as if dead, and my eyes were extremely afflicted with an inflammation, while to crown all these ills, I had a very great difficulty in breathing. I vowed a novena to Saint Francis

---

*According to Catholic theology, the Church Militant is the embattled institution on earth struggling to save souls from the Devil, while the Church Triumphant is God's realm in heaven that receives the souls of those who have died in grace.

Xavier,* and at the same time I was cured. Perhaps God paid regard to the present necessity of our poor Savages, who had need of my assistance. . . .

During the height of the contagious and general malady that afflicted this country, there were two [Indian] Captains, who, with the purpose of corrupting the faith of the young people, offered a sacrifice of three dogs to the Demon, hanging them at the door of their cabin, to ask him for his assistance, and entreat him to stay the course of the contagious disease; but their prayers were not heard, and the undertaking resulted in their own confusion. Two other [Indian] persons, a man and a woman, the one named Pierre and the other Anne, warmly opposed this detestable impiety.

The man, after he had begged them gently to desist, and had recognized that he could not make any impression on their minds, harangued the Youth forcibly in these words: "No, my brothers, there is no question here, either of hunting, or of war, or of Political affairs, regarding which we need listen to these old dreamers, although they are our Elders. It is a question of Prayer, which our [Jesuit] Fathers have taught us. They have never said to us, 'In your afflictions have recourse to the evil Spirit; put your trust in him, and hope for your health from him'; but on the contrary they have taught us that we must have recourse to God, who is the one who governs us, and who alone is able to protect us. Let us then, my brothers, say to him: 'Great God, all-seeing and all-powerful, take pity on us. We wish to die as we have lived. It is you, great God, who are the Master of our lives: if you wish us to die, we consent; but if you wish us to live, give us your assistance.'" The woman added that those who ceased to pray would not only all die, but they would even be the first to die. And so it was; for in three days those two impious ones, who had been well before, were stricken with the disease, which reduced them to such extremity of illness that, after losing their right minds, they strangled themselves with their own hands. Then all the Savages who were in that region divided themselves into two bands. This man and woman also separated, and, although they were very feeble, they ceased not to occupy themselves constantly in visiting the sick and exhorting them to pray, and in preparing them to die well.

From that great desolation, caused by the disease in this country, there have remained, in the minds of the Savages whom I have seen, two things of which they are strongly convinced. The first is, that a great part of the more prominent persons among those who have died of this

---

*A novena is a nine-day sequence of prayers; Francis Xavier (1506–1552) was a Portugese Jesuit and disciple of Ignatius Loyola, the movement's founder, who became known as the "Apostle of the Indies" for his missionary work in India, Southeast Asia, and Japan.

malady have been taken away from this world only to be punished for their infidelity. The second is, that they are all convinced of the necessity of holding firmly to the [Catholic] Faith, and praying better than ever.

NOTES

1. Russell Thornton, Jonathan Warren, and Tim Miller, "Depopulation in the Southeast after 1492," in *Disease and Demography in the Americas,* eds. John W. Verano and Douglas H. Ubelaker (Washington DC: Smithsonian Institution Press, 1992), 191; Noble David Cook, "Disease and the Depopulation of Hispaniola, 1492–1518," *Colonial Latin American Review* 2 (1993): 236; Suzanne Austin Alchon, *A Pest in the Land: New World Epidemics in a Global Perspective* (Albuquerque, NM: University of New Mexico Press, 2003), 63–64.

2. Sherburne F. Cook, "Significance of Disease in the Extinction of the New England Indian," *Human Biology* 45 (1973): 493.

3. Thomas M. Whitmore, *Disease and Death in Early Colonial Mexico: Stimulating Amerindian Depopulation* (Boulder, CO: Westview Press, 1992), 208.

4. Alchon, *A Pest in the Land,* 2–5, 143–145.

5. *The Annals of the Cakchiquels,* trans. Adrián Recinos and Delia Goetz (Norman, OK: University of Oklahoma Press, 1953), 116.

6. *The Book of Chilam Balam of Chumayel,* ed. Ralph L. Roys (Norman, OK: University of Oklahoma Press, 1967), 83.

7. *The Bernal Díaz Chronicles: The True Story of the Conquest of Mexico,* trans. and ed. Albert Idell (Garden City, NY: Doubleday and Co., 1956), 405.

8. Charles Francis Adams, *Three Episodes of Massachusetts History,* 2 vols. (Boston and New York: Houghton, Mifflin and Co., 1892), 1: 11.

9. Increase Mather, *A Relation of the Troubles which have Hapned in New-England, by Reason of the Indians There* (Boston: John Foster, 1677), 23.

10. *The Jesuit Relations and Allied Documents,* ed. Reuben G. Thwaites, 73 vols. (Cleveland: Burrows Brothers, 1896–1900), 3: 105.

11. Ibid., 19: 91–93.

CHAPTER

3

Disease and the Birth of Modern Medicine: Bubonic and Pneumonic Plague in India and China, 1896–1921

THE PLAGUE BREAKS OUT IN INDIA

In August or September of 1896, bubonic plague called at the port of Bombay, one of the major shipping hubs in the British colony of India. Although plague had established a centuries-old foothold in the Himalayan borderlands of northeastern India – an endemic center from which it struck out into the surrounding countryside at least once a decade throughout the nineteenth century – the disease probably came to Bombay by steamship from the British-held port of Hong Kong, where bubonic plague had broken out two years earlier in 1894. Other Indian cities soon followed Bombay as centers of plague, and by the century's end, plague had a firm grip on the countryside, particularly in the northern and western regions, where the vast majority of the plague deaths occurred. By 1930, India's death toll from the plague was at least 12 million, of which half had occurred in the decade between 1898 and 1908. India's plague totals during these years comprised 95 percent of the world's mortality from the disease.

THE BRITISH RAJ'S RESPONSE

The British government's response to this epidemic was unique in that it was perhaps the most concerted effort ever undertaken to date in order to combat a disease. In early 1897, the Epidemic Diseases Act was rushed through the viceroy's council, giving the government unfettered powers to inspect and detain ship, road, and rail passengers suspected of carrying plague; to segregate and hospitalize plague victims, suspects, or contacts in any city, town, or village throughout India; to conduct searches of any dwelling thought to harbor plague victims and to disinfect, air out, or even demolish such dwellings; to evacuate whole towns if necessary of their populations to temporary health camps; and to prohibit fairs and pilgrimages where plague carriers may congregate and spread the disease. At least initially, these measures were often carried out by army officers and their troops.

Aside from an altruistic desire to serve the health needs of its subjects, the British government undoubtedly had more self-serving motives to take the measures that it did. The preservation of its lucrative trade within and without India was a high priority for the government. Another important consideration, from the British point of view, was the political dimension of their response to the plague crisis. A generation earlier, in 1857, the British had faced the Sepoy Rebellion, which shook British rule in India to the core. Some Civil Service officials, such as W.L. Reade, Chief Plague Authority of Pune, regarded plague as "one of the best opportunities for riveting our rule in India, as it is not only an opportunity for showing a kindness to the people, but also for showing the superiority of our Western Science, and thoroughness" (see Reade's letter in the sources below). Finally, the historical factor should not be neglected, as the European response to modern plague was heavily influenced by its experience with the Black Death during the medieval and early modern eras (see Chapter 1). British authorities in India clearly identified their present plague crisis as created by the same disease thought responsible for the Black Death. Victorians' fear of plague was ably exploited by Sir Arthur Conan Doyle in one of his Sherlock Holmes stories,

"The Giant Rat of Sumatra," in which Holmes' evil arch-rival, Professor Moriarity, tries to import the disease into London through what, the Indian Plague Commission had revealed, was its main animal carrier.

THE BLACK DEATH AND THE INDIAN PLAGUE

An indisputable benefit of the colonial government's overwhelming response to plague was an impressive accumulation of data on the disease. These data were first presented in several reports on the Bombay plague published between 1897 and 1900 and in the *Minutes of Evidence* and *Report* published by the Indian Plague Commission in 1900–1901. Later this was supplemented by annual articles published by the Commission in the *Journal of Hygiene* between 1906 and 1937. It is tempting to regard this outpouring of evidence as the definitive authority against which all occurrences of the disease in all places and times should be measured. Recently one scholar has used the Indian evidence to reject identification of the medieval Black Death with modern plague, on the contention that the former occurrence of the disease does not conform in recorded symptomology and epidemiological behavior with the later outbreak in turn-of-the-century India.[1] Nonetheless, it is perhaps significant that no alternative disease has yet been proposed that better fits the historical descriptions of the Black Death better than plague.

This controversy aside, there are some striking parallels in at least the social circumstances of the victims of both the Black Death and the Indian plague. Witness after witness before the Indian Plague Commission described the typical plague venues as poorly ventilated, unsanitary, overcrowded mud and thatch dwellings which lacked indoor plumbing, housed grain and domesticated animals as well as humans, were closely spaced together, and, above all, were infested with rats, all characteristics that could equally well apply to the peasant hovels and urban houses of fourteenth-century Europe. Even the tragic stories of abandonment of family members told by Giovanni Boccaccio and other chroniclers of the medieval Black Death (Chapter 1) find an eerie echo in the testimony before the Indian Plague Commission. Colonel Donald Robertson, Resident of the Mysore State, told the Commission that the fear of plague was so great at Bangalore "that one of the most deplorable results of the epidemic perhaps is the absence of natural affection displayed in a great many cases. Mothers have refused to nurse their children and frequently people have left their sick relatives in a house and gone away." Major G.E. Hyde-Cates, Political Agent of Cutch, confirmed that fear of plague led people to flee their homes with sick relations inside, who were left to die until their bodies were discovered by the authorities. There were also tales in Bangalore and Bombay of how plague went hand in hand with a break-down in morality and religious observance. Even the overarching theme of native resistance to plague controls in India finds a striking parallel in Italy's experience with the Black Death during the seventeenth century.

EVIDENCE COLLECTION AND ANALYSIS

It would be a mistake to assume that the Indian government's evidence on plague can be taken as purely scientific fact; as is true of any histori-cal document, it must be viewed within its contemporary context. Especially with regard to the early evidence compiled before 1900, the government's efforts at data collection were often hampered by the lack of cooperation, and at times downright hostility, of the native subjects who comprised the vast majority of the plague victims. The government desperately tried to convince its skeptical native subjects to notify the authorities of any plague victims in their homes in order to remove and isolate them from the rest of the population, but as the Indian Plague Commission frankly admitted, government hospitals were "everywhere unpopular" and people displayed "a vague fear and detestation" of them. The "unreasoning terror" of natives at the very "idea of going to hospital" was only natural considering that death rates from plague in these venues were extremely high, ranging from 60 percent in Bangalore to 80 percent in Calcutta. This was explained as owing to the fact that only "moribund" patients on the verge of death were removed to hospital; those still healthy or recovering from plague naturally enough associated hospitals with dying rather than healing, since nothing really could be done to cure patients of the plague. In terms of taking hospital statistics as evidence of transmission, what this means is that only a very select group of patients served as the basis of the government's study of plague's contagiousness.

There were plenty of other weaknesses to the government's attempts to scientifically study plague. Aside from collecting data from patients in hospital, the government also relied on compiling statistics from the morgue. Yet the Commission was forced to conclude that corpse inspection was a defective measure that should be abandoned, since it was extremely unpopular among the masses, so that many cases went unreported and were even concealed from authorities, and since true cases of plague were difficult to detect, even for qualified medical officers, let alone the volunteers whom the government usually employed. Similar difficulties were encountered in trying to diagnose the living; indeed, one medical authority in Pune estimated that less than half of plague victims had reported themselves as sick before they died. It also should be noted that, up until at least 1901, the Indian Plague Commission still did not understand how bubonic plague was spread from rats to humans; despite the fact that a French microbiologist, Paul-Louis Simond, had in 1898 enunciated the theory that fleas might be responsible, the Commission roundly rejected the notion as "hardly deserving of consideration." Ironically, the one person to entertain the idea that fleas could spread plague was a lowly hospital assistant in the Kaira district, who observed "swarms of fleas" in the houses and streets of every village infected. The Commission also continued to entertain other erroneous speculations, such as that plague bacilli entered the body through the digestive tract or through the soles of feet in contact with infected earthen floors. These theories inevitably influenced how the Commission approached the study of plague.

INITIAL COLONIAL POLICY AND NATIVE RESISTANCE

For most scholars, the significance of plague in India is to be found not in its biological aspects, but in its impact upon Britain's colonial policy on the subcontinent at the end of the nineteenth century. However ambitious and well intentioned its policy, the government's determination to introduce Western science and medicine to its Indian colony soon ran headlong into the stonewall of native customs, traditions, and religious beliefs. Perhaps most disconcerting to a Civil Service hoping to demonstrate the enlightened benevolence of its rule in India, native subjects came to associate plague measures "with torture and death, not with health and healing."[2] Indeed, many of those on the front lines of the epidemic testified before the Indian Plague Commission that the measures, when rigidly enforced without consideration for native sensibilities, contributed more to the problem than the cure. Lieutenant W.J. Niblock of the Indian Medical Service testified that the very act of removing patients from their homes did them harm, citing one case in Karachi where the patient's chances of recovery were reduced by 50 percent after arrival at hospital. The fact that a high number of cases died at hospital also led people to believe "that when a man goes to the Plague Hospital he goes there to die." A native pleader in Satara even claimed that the very mention of being taken to hospital caused a patient to expire on the spot. Other unintended effects of plague measures were the fact that residents often helped spread the infection when they fled their homes or concealed cases in other people's homes in order to avoid hospitalization or segregation, while disinfection may also have helped propagate rather than contain the disease by forcing infected rats and other plague carriers elsewhere.

Several officials testified that what people feared above all were the government's efforts to combat the plague, in equal or even greater measure to the disease itself. When asked which measure natives feared the most, witnesses often cited segregation, since it separated family members from sick relatives whom they might never see again and often failed to respect caste systems, while inspection of both living and dead plague patients offended Hindu and Muslim religious feelings. House searches and disinfection were also highly unpopular, for numerous reasons: invasion of privacy, causing the destruction of personal property or structural damage to the dwelling, even the belief that disinfectants were harmful to human health (as perchloride mercury, in fact, was) or were simply ineffective. The humiliation that a house search and disinfection could entail to its owner is well illustrated by the testimony of Captain C.H. James, Deputy Sanitary Commissioner of the Punjab, who described the procedure at Lahore. The owner of the house was made to sit in the street while a gang of "coolies" pumped a stream of antiseptic solution throughout the interior until the ceiling, walls, and floor were dripping wet. All the furniture and salvageable property were then carried out to dry in the sun, while rubbish and rags were burnt out in the open. No wonder natives went to elaborate lengths to evade the authorities, such as substituting healthy people for sick ones in roll-calls, hiding corpses in dust heaps or walling up infected clothes, and inducing native doctors to diagnose victims as suffering from asthma or bronchitis instead of plague. The only measure on which all could agree was effective in combating the spread of

FIGURE 3.1   A Hospital.   A plague hospital in Bombay, India. The bubonic plague first came to Bombay from Hong Kong in August–September 1896. The wheeled stretcher was used to convey vicitims to the hospital, but the attendants do not wear masks, unlike those during the pneumonic plague outbreak in Manchuria. This photo was taken in 1922, when the plague was still raging in India.

sickness was evacuation of the affected area, which was often done voluntarily by the natives themselves in accordance with their time-honored customs.

That native resistance to plague measures had to be taken seriously was impressed upon British authorities' minds by, among other disturbances, the riot attack on October 29, 1896 upon the government's Arthur Road Infectious Diseases Hospital in Bombay, and by the assassination on June 22, 1897 of W.C. Rand, chairman of the Plague Committee in Pune, who was known for his draconian enforcement of measures as well as his contempt for "native agency." Native newspaper reports not only confirmed what the Indian Plague Commission discovered, that measures such as hospitalization and segregation rode roughshod over people's familial and religious concerns, but also that, more alarmingly, they had given rise to "plague rumors." These included suspicions of poisoning of native patients by British medical staff, looting of possessions and forcible seizure of persons for extortion purposes, compulsory inoculation, even the possibility that plague hospitals cut up native bodies in order to extract a healing balm known as *momiai*. If there was no truth to these charges, they at least pointed to the complete failure of the government to capture the gratitude and goodwill of its subjects for whom it was purportedly carrying out its extraordinary measures. One scholar has characterized the collective impact of all these rumors, riots, and other rumblings of alienation as "the greatest upsurge of public resistance to Western medicine and sanitation that nineteenth-century India had witnessed," to the point that it "represented a profound crisis for Western medicine and for the power of the colonial state."[3]

NEW POLICIES

By 1898–1899, many in the Civil Service had come round to the realization that, what may have started out as a medical problem – to contain the spread of plague both within and without India – had now become a full-blown political crisis. From the viceroy down, it was acknowledged that a new policy of conciliation and accommodation was needed to address the now higher priority of political stability, and indeed if the government's plague measures were to have any effect at all. The new strategy included the modification, and even complete abandonment, of the previous measures of hospitalization, segregation, disinfection, and corpse inspection. In some localities, plague contacts were allowed to remain in their homes provided they were inoculated, while disinfection with chemicals was reduced to simple ventilation or was done privately. Corpse inspection could also be avoided if certificates were obtained that showed patients had been examined in life. Above all, native agency was now adopted as a vital intermediary between the people and the government. Traditional healers, Hindu *vaids* and Muslim *hakims*, could serve as official medical inspectors and doctors, while house searches were carried out by "native gentlemen" and sepoys (native troops). A ward system with native volunteers was given responsibility for segregation and evacuation in the cities, while tribal headmen carried out this duty in the villages. Health camps were also made more permissive and voluntary, with families no longer separated and the people able to go back and forth to their homes and businesses during the day, provided they did not stay overnight. Relatives and friends were allowed to attend patients in hospital, and more choice was given with regard to hospitalization, to include caste and local ward hospitals where native customs were respected.

LESSONS LEARNED

India's turn-of-the-century plague experience clearly demonstrated the limits of colonial medicine in the face of native tradition and resistance. When married to coercive imperialism, Western medicine could not earn the trust of its native patients and therefore became a less-than-effective remedy. This does not mean, however, that progress was not made in improving public health in India. Moreover, some Civil Service officers had the best interests of their native charges at heart and were flexible enough to compromise when confronted with opposition to originally stringent measures. Nor was the native response monolithic. It is true that the vast majority of native witnesses before the Indian Plague Commission were strongly in favor of mollification of plague measures, and they could be defensive of their compatriots' refusal to obey the rules, even when these were mitigated. But a notable exception to this rule was Dr. U.L. Desai, consulting physician to the plague hospital in Nasik, who had received all his medical education in England and Scotland and who testified before the Commission on March 14, 1899. When asked by the Commission to recommend a "plan of campaign against plague," Dr. Desai gave this remarkable answer:

> Battle against plague has to be waged not only as against a specific disease, but as against general causes of unhealthiness leading to lowered vitality of the masses, and consequent increased mortality. It will have to be a huge war against the continued forces of hereditary habits, religious prejudices, conserved customs, and extreme ignorance of the laws of personal, social, and public hygiene, which go to make up the social life of an Asiatic. It is to be a thorough meeting of the sanitary and medical needs of the country by numerous compulsory enactments of the country, by numerous compulsory enactments and institutions, which shall be bitter pills for the masses of India to swallow, and unless that is done, plague germs shall find fit nidus to grow, multiply, and cause ravages in various parts of India.[4]

This went beyond even the ambitions of British Civil Servants. Indeed, Dr. Desai proceeded to recommend very far-reaching and permanent measures to combat future outbreaks of plague, to include improvements in sewage systems, better housing, educational schemes to promote hygiene, and compulsory registration of all medical practitioners, directed particularly at native *vaids* and *hakims*. When asked if he thought the country was ready for "such a large measure," Dr. Desai again responded with some barely concealed contempt for the "ignorant masses," who had previously practiced suttee (widow immolation) and infanticide until these were suppressed with "strong measures." For Desai, the "will of the people is not to be taken into consideration, but their welfare," because real cause of plague "lies hidden under lies, quackery, and superstition." Although Desai had to concede that many of the common people continue to favor their *vaids* and *hakims* on religious grounds, he was confident that they would eventually turn to European medicine. Assuredly, Dr. Desai and other middle-class Indians like him were thinking not just in terms of healthier patients. Modernization along European lines was for them not only the most potent weapon against plague, but also the surest road to an independent India.

THE PLAGUE BREAKS OUT IN MANCHURIA

The other major case of plague in Asia at the dawn of the twentieth century presents both intriguing parallels and differences with the experience in India. During the winters of 1910–1911 and 1920–1921, a severe outbreak of pneumonic plague struck Manchuria. The first epidemic swept away as much as 60,000 inhabitants throughout Manchuria and North China, while the second is estimated to have carried off 8,500 in primarily North Manchuria and East Siberia. While India's epidemic was overwhelmingly bubonic in character (less than 3 percent of cases were of the pneumonic variety), the outbreak in Manchuria was in equal measure dominated by primary plague pneumonia and therefore involved different symptoms, methods of transmission, virulence, and rates of mortality. Pneumonic plague's distinctive symptom, absent the buboes of bubonic plague, is the coughing up of a thin, bloody sputum, sometimes in such quantities that "the floor and bedding are covered with blood."[5] As we saw in Chapter 1, whereas bubonic plague patients might take up to a week to die, pneumonic victims are dead in typically 2–3 days; and while a significant percentage of bubonic patients recover naturally from the disease, there are hardly no survivors of pneumonic attacks. Pneumonic plague is also distinctive in its form of transmission, owing largely to the airborne emissions of bacteria in droplet suspension emitted by the patient when coughing; experiments conducted in the plague wards at Harbin, Manchuria, in 1920–1921 found that expectorated sputum was infective up to five feet away. Thus, whereas bubonic plague is a disease spread to humans through rats and fleas, pneumonic plague involves primarily a human-to-human agency. All these factors impacted how Chinese authorities in Manchuria responded to the plague relative to the British approach in India.

As we also saw in Chapter 1, plague is endemic to the Mongolian and Manchurian steppes, probably established in the thirteenth century, when Mongol armies possibly brought the disease back from a campaign in the Himalayan region of Yunnan and Burma. Russian and Chinese bacteriologists established that the Siberian marmot or tarabagan rodents native to Manchuria were susceptible to both bubonic and pneumonic plague and that they hosted fleas (*Ceratophyllus silantievi*) that harbored the plague bacilli. The early decades of the twentieth century saw an explosion of interest in the trade of tarabagan fur, which was used as a cheap substitute for sable and mink, and as a consequence, many more humans came into contact with tarabagans in the form of inexpert trappers and handlers of their skins. By 1910–1911, two million tarabagan skins were being exported from Manchuria annually, and the price per skin had risen to the extent that three months' hunting could realize as much pay as a whole year from other occupations, thus attracting as many as 11,000 Chinese peasants – who had little knowledge or experience in handling the animals – to the trade. Whereas bubonic plague epidemics in humans go hand-in-hand with epizootics, or incidents of the disease among rodents such as the tarabagan, the pneumonic outbreaks in Manchuria are thought to have been triggered by its occurrence as a secondary symptom of bubonic plague already present in the human population. Nonetheless, the possibility of plague pneumonia being spread directly from animal to human cannot be discounted. Social and environmental conditions in some cities of Manchuria during the winters of 1910–1911 and 1920–1921 were ideal for the human-to-human contagion required for the spread of pneumonic plague. The inns of Manchouli, the western-most city of Manchuria from which tarabagan furs were exported, were largely underground dwellings containing very few windows, where guest hunters ate and slept in conditions resembling a ship's cargo for slaves: in one inn, three tiers of bunks harboring up to 40 berths were crammed within a space just 15 by 12 feet square. It was noted in 1911 that no partitions existed between adjoining berths, so that the occupants "can easily breathe and cough into each other's faces."[6] The coal mines of Dalainor, a town just to the east of Manchouli where pneumonic plague broke out in January 1921, provided similarly ideal conditions for spread of an airborne disease; here miners likewise lived in underground barracks, with only one or two glass windows set in the roof, where they ate and slept on long wooden biers with no partitions between occupants and where as many as 80 men crowded into a space 20 by 60 feet square.

GOVERNMENTAL RESPONSE

Just as bubonic plague did in British India, the outbreak of such a deadly disease as pneumonic plague provoked the Manchu government of China to respond with forceful, and sometimes unpopular, measures to combat its continuation and spread. Plague had been making its way across Manchuria from the Russian border since September of 1910, but it was not until December, when a dozen cases a day were being reported from Harbin, the main railway and shipping hub for the province, that the Foreign Office in Peking dispatched a Cambridge-trained Chinese doctor, Wu Liande, to investigate. With the approval of the government, Dr. Wu implemented measures such as quarantine, hospitalization of plague patients, segregation of contacts, evacuation of inhabitants, and disinfection of homes that were likewise carried out by the British in India. But because of the uniquely infectious character of pneumonic plague, Dr. Wu also established protocols, such as the wearing of cotton-gauze masks and head-to-toe protective garb by all medical attendants and the mass cremation of plague corpses, which had not been widely adopted in India. As in India, Dr. Wu and his staff encountered some resistance and opposition from the native population to his efforts to introduce modern Western ideas of sanitation and medicine. How this played out in Chinese Manchuria during the second decade of the twentieth century will be explored below.

SOURCES

Bubonic Plague in Pune, India: The Native Response

Among all the official documents and reports produced by the British government during the bubonic plague crisis in India, the voices of natives who were, after all, the chief victims of the disease are often lost or simply unrecorded. Some natives did testify before the Indian Plague Commission, but they were invariably involved in some way with the government's efforts to combat the disease, either as members of a plague commission, as health officers, or as volunteers. Although they did not always agree with the government's measures, their testimony can hardly be considered representative. Scholars have instead turned to native newspapers, whose articles were distilled and compiled in reports to the India Office, in order to find reliable and authentic witnesses to the native perspective.

This is not to say that native newspapers do not have their own biases and drawbacks as a source of historical information on the plague in India. They were generally representative of the educated Indian middle class, who could be as contemptuous of the "ignorant masses" as the British. They also had to walk a fine line between catering to their native readers and not offending the watchful eyes of the British government. Also, there was a wide variety of political opinions and alignments among Indian newspapers. Most were critical of the government's unprecedented measures that generally went against native customs and religious beliefs. But some sided with Western science and medicine as the only effective way to combat plague. For example, while most native newspapers came out against the Epidemic Diseases Act of 1897, the *Sanjivani* remarked that, while the act "may prove oppressive in isolated cases, . . . the good that it will do to the public will far outweigh the evil which is likely to result from it." The *Kaiser-e-Hind* in Karachi supported plague measures such as segregation and isolation because it believed these would keep plague from spreading, while in Bombay, both the *Arunodaya* and the *Bombay Samáchár* urged their readers to submit to the "supreme necessities" of hospitalization and disinfection, even if this should mean putting up with "hardships" like the destruction of their houses and property. Two Muslim papers in Bombay, *Akhbár-e-Islám* and the *Muslim Herald,* scolded the "selfish and ignorant persons" and "malcontents of the Muhammadan community" who were stirring up the people against the Plague Committee and hindering it from doing its work, such as segregation and house-to-house searches, since these measures were in the people's own best interests.

Nonetheless, newspapers did provide an alternative viewpoint from that of the government, and nowhere is this demonstrated more clearly than in the case of R.A.L. Moore, an Indian Civil Service officer and collector of Surat who was in charge of plague operations there. In his testimony before the Indian Plague Commission on March 8, 1899, Moore stated that he allowed the different castes to start their own hospitals in the city, provided they paid for their own expenses. It is not until one reads the local newspapers for Surat that one learns that, in fact, Moore had apparently forbidden the formation of caste hospitals early in 1897 on the excuse that the Civil Surgeon could not supervise them all. It was also alleged that Moore had no regard for the natives' various religious sympathies, which included Hindu, Parsi, and both Sunni and Shia Muslim adherents. Moore was so unpopular in Surat that it was said that he had to bring out a military escort in order to "overawe the populace" and that everyone was looking forward to his transfer to Nasik, which eventually did occur in May 1898.

Native newspapers' concern with the British government's policy against plague began with the publication of the Epidemic Diseases Act in February 1897. Many papers accurately predicted that the government would encounter bitter and widespread opposition to its planned measures. The *Burdwan Sanjivani* was especially concerned about segregation, asking, in the hypothetical case of a child attacked by plague, "How will its parents take it if it is forcibly removed to a hospital?" Although the government might answer that its measures, while painful for the individual, are necessary for the general welfare, the paper responded that "few will desire to live in a country where the wife is separated from the husband, the child from the parent, and the parent from the child. We call this selfishness, and not self-sacrifice." The *Hitavadi* saw sinister signs in that the act could theoretically be used on the occasion of any disease outbreak, not just plague, which would inevitably lead to oppression and "despotic powers" wielded by the government. The *Bangavasi* was exercised over the fact that cultural values alien to the natives were being forced upon them: "Why prevent the helpless and long suffering Hindu from dying in peace? When death summons us we must die. Why disturb and distract us in the name of science?"

When the measures did come into effect, native newspapers naturally were not slow to record the uproar that ensued. Paper after paper emphasized that what caused panic and fear in the populace was not the plague itself, but the *zulum*, or oppression, occasioned by the government's very efforts to combat the spread of the disease. Such measures were especially resented when they seemed to have no effect and the plague came back in increased virulence, or when wrongful diagnoses were made of hospitalized patients. Another sore point recorded by the papers was that plague committees, whose powers superseded those of local municipal councils, were composed entirely of Europeans; natives were nowhere represented. Particularly ominous for a British Civil Servant reading these reports must have been the fact that Hindus and Muslims were joining forces to protest measures that offended native religious sensibilities, such as the *purdah*, or sexual modesty of females. Several papers raised the specter of the 1857 Mutiny in order to impress upon readers the volatility of the political implications of the government's plague policy. Also disheartening for government officials must have been to read accounts of wild rumors spreading among the native public regarding what was happening in hospitals. Although most papers discounted such rumors as groundless, they did document cases of theft and violation of shrines during house-to-house searches and of the wrongful diagnosis and removal to hospital of suspected plague victims.

Pune presents a special case, since measures there were perhaps the most rigorous in all of India. The plague apparently first struck Pune in December 1896. It then died down by the end of May 1897, but struck again in late July and August 1897 and lasted until February 1898. In March 1897, a Plague Committee was set up, chaired by an Indian Civil Service officer, W.C. Rand. Among the most hated measures enacted by Rand and the Committee was the sending round of British soldiers, dubbed by native newspapers as the "white bulls" or "Tommy Atkins," to inspect houses for suspected plague victims: reports came in of soldiers destroying and pilfering property, violating sanctuaries and idols, making obscene gestures toward women, and even forcing some to strip naked and perform humiliating exercises or dances. Almost equally offensive was the report that Rand turned a deaf ear to native petitions and complaints, or that he refused to allow "native agency" to play any meaningful role in his measures, such as by allowing native gentlemen to direct house-to-house searches. By April of 1897, newspaper rhetoric had built to a feverish pitch. *Dnyán Prakásh* charged the Plague Committee with tyrannizing the people of Pune "for tyranny's sake – for no other reason save that the members of that body take a peculiar delight in making the citizens feel their power." *Kalpataru* went so far as to say that "the plague authorities are simply butchers who are torturing and harassing the inhabitants of Poona in the name of sanitary science." Some papers appealed to Britain's own history to justify resistance to their present oppression, such as Magna Carta or the defeat of the Spanish Armada, while others likened their sufferings to those under the Inquisition or the Reign of Terror during the French Revolution. *Dnyán Prakásh* predicted that future English historians of the plague in Pune would damn Rand for having brought a "sense of shame" to the history of their nation.

Rand's regime appeared especially oppressive when compared to that of General W.F. Gatacre in nearby Bombay, who took a much more open view toward native agency and whose tact and willingness to compromise won him the gratitude of the city, which proposed raising a monument in his honor. In the end, an assassin's bullet settled the matter on June 22, 1897. Based on its own reports, the government seemed justified in shutting down native presses in retaliation for Rand's murder. Since the beginning of April, various newspapers had been taunting their readers for their "cowardly" submission to humiliating plague measures – particularly the seizure of property, destruction of sacred images, and manhandling of women. But the aftermath of Rand's assassination was also the occasion for some self-reflection among the city's native editors. While not exonerating Rand, the *Vártáhar* nonetheless pointed to the people's complicity in concealing plague cases and heartlessly dumping dead relatives in the city's streets, and the paper blamed the Hindu nationalist leader, Bal Gangadhar Tilak (editor of another Pune newspaper, the *Mahrátta*), for exploiting native sentiment for his own naked political aims.

While the government successfully used plague as an opportunity to increase its stranglehold over a dangerously independent municipal council in Pune, it also was forced to make some concessions with regard to its plague policy. By the time the second epidemic hit in August 1897, the Plague Committee under Rand's successor, R.A. Lamb, was ready to make some modifications in its inspection measures, as editorials from the newspapers *Kesari* and

Dnyán Prakásh of September 28 and 30, which are excerpted below, bear witness. Conditions in the segregation camp also were improved. The governor of Bombay, Lord Sandhurst, who had a reputation for browbeating Indian Brahmins for their "persistent criticism of British policies," inaugurated a new spirit of "cooperation" by visiting Pune in September and holding a meeting with native leaders in the Council Hall, where he actually solicited suggestions. While all this was highly praised in native newspapers, they continued to register complaints, such as a violation of a temple by one of the medical inspectors and the continued insolence shown by British soldiers to native volunteers. The *Kesari* and *Dnyán Prakásh* had plenty of suggestions for further concessions by the government (see below). But compared to what had gone before, any show of compromise was bound to be considered an improvement.

■ Newspaper Reports, February–September 1897

The following excerpts are from British reports on five native newspapers in Pune during the city's first plague epidemic in the winter and spring of 1897 and at the start of its second epidemic by the late summer and autumn of that year. The reports are summaries of the original articles and were compiled by the British government in order to monitor the newspapers, which were important barometers of native sentiment. In this instance, the newspaper reports are particularly revealing about how natives were responding to the notoriously rigorous measures enacted by Pune's Plague Committee, chaired by W.C. Rand. Even though they are second hand, the reports are a valuable and accessible source on the native perspective of the plague in India.

As you read these accounts, you will quickly see that conspiracy theories are not unique to our day or culture. What were the popular rumors that ran through India? Do any of them seem credible? Which ones? Conspiracy theories aside, why were early British efforts at plague suppression met with such resistance, and how did the colonial government attempt to correct those errors? Did British plague policies apparently strengthen or weaken Great Britain's hand in India?

Source: British Library, L/R/5/152, India Office Records Neg. 18105.

Poona Vaibhav, February 21: In every place where the Government is taking measures against the bubonic plague, the people feel as if they are being oppressed by Government. In Poona [Pune], too, we are experiencing the effect of these plague preventive measures, such as the removal of tiles from buildings, destruction of stored grain, compelling even healthy persons to go to hospital, etc. We are even told that, among other things, ornaments are burnt and that in one case a person suffering from an ordinary inflammation of the parotid glands was compulsorily removed to the hospital. Is this humanity or [concern for the] public good or [a means of] sweeping off the subject population? To compulsorily separate a helpless sick person from his relations is meaner than [the acts of] a butcher, and if Government will do it we cannot say what the effect of it will be on the minds of the populace. In some villages the people have come to think that the Sarkar [government], finding its subjects unmanageable, is devising means to reduce their number. They say that it mixes poison in opium. They even hesitate to accept the dole of bread distributed in the famine camps under the belief that poison is mixed with the bread. They think that the hospitals are now under the management of new doctors who put poison into the medicines. These are undoubtedly the idle imaginings of foolish brains, but it is not desirable that the people should come to entertain such notions about Government. It is not a good sign that the old firmly rooted belief that the Sarkar is the *mabap* [mother–father] of the people, that it protects them and redresses their grievances, should disappear. If Government under such circumstances will oppress people in the shape of plague preventive measures and pass laws giving ample powers to their officers to carry them out, there is every probability that the Government and the people will be the bitterest enemies of each other.

Vyápári, February 21: The measures that are at present being taken at Poona for the suppression of the plague, such as the limewashing of houses, the destruction of huts, the compulsory segregation of plague patients, are to our mind indications of nothing but folly and madness. These may be the most approved means, according to western sanitary science, of stamping out the plague, but it will be very difficult to persuade an orthodox Native to believe in their efficacy. Our people, who are brought up in the old order of ideas, generally look upon such epidemic diseases as the result of Divine displeasure and so they seek to suppress them by offering oblations to the Deity and so forth. We consider the effort of the executive to be so much misdirection of energy and feel inclined to laugh at them for their folly. The thing is that no one knows anything for certain about the plague and the proper means of suppressing it. . . . If that be so, why create uneasiness and discontent in the minds of the people by forcibly removing sick persons from their houses? The moral effect of segregation alone, apart from the character of the arrangements at the segregation hospital, is sufficient to retard the recovery of a patient compulsorily removed from among his relations. We hope, therefore, that the local authorities who are vested with ample powers for dealing with the plague will not fail to take into consideration this seriously unsettling effect of compulsory segregation on the minds of an orthodox populace and will shape their measures with tact, prudence and commonsense.

Poona Vaibhav, April 11: The people of Poona are so much disgusted with the preventive measures taken in the city that they would rather die of the plague than have to submit to the *zulum* of Government. People in robust health are causelessly dragged to the prison-like cells by the soldiers, and there the poor wretches sometimes die of panic, heat or hunger. History presents no example of such oppression on the subjects of any ruler. A child of 5 or 6 years may be suffering from slight fever, but if the party of soldiers declare it to be suffering from the plague, it is at once separated from its parents in spite of its piteous cries and entreaties not to be taken away from under the parental roof. A husband is separated from his wife and aged persons from their relations. The lives and property of the people are being ruined and disgust is being produced in their minds. It is a pity that the Government officers do not realise all this. The authorities say that the preventive measures are being taken in the interests of the people themselves, but unfortunately the people do not take the same view of the matter. The people are loyal and submissive and do not offer resistance to the authorities in their plague measures, but it will never do to oppress them. There are examples in Indian history of oppressive *regimés* being overthrown through agencies sent by God for the deliverance of the oppressed. We request the authorities to bear such historical examples in mind and to be cautious in enforcing their plague measures.

Mahrátta, July 25: We assert that it is entirely due to Mr. Rand that the Natives could not be of any great use. In the first place, Mr. Rand did neither solicit nor encourage Native help. He would rather dispense with Native agency as he looked upon it as an incumbrance and had no faith in its honest working. This will be proved by the fact that he, even when the plague had almost subsided, could not bring himself to trust licensed and respectable medical practitioners to honestly certify deaths in the city. It is also notorious that those Native gentlemen who did volunteer themselves in spite of Mr. Rand's cold discouragement had to withdraw disgusted and insulted at the hands of those models of politeness so much applauded by the Anglo-Indian press, the British soldiers, and also their officers, who did not show themselves much better. There are instances of highly respectable Native volunteers being insulted by those in charge of search parties. "Mind your business: it is simply to attend and not to speak," was the courteous reply vouchsafed to those who protested against a healthy man being seized, a sick man ill-treated, or property being wantonly destroyed. If under these circumstances the Natives were not of much use, it is evidently because Mr. Rand did not want them to be.

Kesari and *Dnyán Prakásh,* September 28 and 30: It is a very pleasing sign of the times that His Excellency the Governor seems to have profited by past experience in the matter of taking measures for stamping out the plague in Poona. His Excellency called together the leaders of Native opinion in Poona at the Council Hall and patiently heard their views about the most suitable measures for the suppression of the plague. It is quite right that both the people and the Government should co-operate together in a friendly manner in driving out the plague. It has been arranged to organise search parties for discovering plague cases and they are to consist of one British soldier, two Native sepoys and one Native volunteer in charge. It was made a matter of common complaint on the last occasion, when the plague was in our midst, that the volunteers who accompanied the search parties had no authority and that they were very often treated with contempt. The present arrangement removes this complaint by investing the volunteers with defined authority and by entrusting the sole conduct of the parties to them. It has also been ruled that the British soldier accompanying the search party is to take no part in the search itself, but that he is to be posted outside the house while the actual work of searching the houses is being done by his Native comrades. This is also a distinct improvement, as the Native soldiers are expected to be conversant with Native customs and thus to show proper respect to Native prejudices in the matter of religion, etc. [but] we do not see why there should be even one British soldier with every search party. Is he included for the purpose of striking terror into the minds of the people? If that be the object, we can say that the presence of the European soldier is sure to achieve it, because the people have conceived a great dread of the soldiers. Segregation of the healthy from the sick is now demonstrated to be the only way of suppressing the plague, but great care ought to be taken to leave no unnecessary ground of complaint to the people in enforcing segregation. People suffering from other diseases than the plague should not be taken to the plague hospital. House-owners, before being segregated with their families, should be given every facility to make arrangements regarding their property during their absence. Women should on no account be made to stand out of the houses, and should be examined and nursed by female doctors and female attendants respectively. Patients should be at liberty to be treated by their own doctors and the persons in the segregation camp should be allowed to take food, provisions, etc., from their houses. Rich persons, owning gardens outside the city, should be allowed to segregate their families there. The leaders of Native society should not flee from the city in a panic, but remain at their posts and take upon themselves the duties of volunteers. This is a fine opportunity for them to show that Natives are as capable of managing these things as Europeans and that they do possess the organizing and administrative tact.

Bubonic Plague in Pune, India: The Official Response

In response to the first outbreak of plague in Pune that began in December 1896, the British government in India set up a Plague Committee for the city in March 1897. Already in September 1896, when it was known that the plague had come to Bombay, less than 200 miles away, the local municipal government of Pune began inspecting railway passengers entering the city, although no provision was made as yet for hospitalization or segregation of suspected plague victims. An Indian Civil Service Officer, W.C. Rand, was placed in charge of the Committee as its chairman. Rand was apparently heavily influenced by an officer in the Army Medical Service, Surgeon-Captain W.W.O. Beveridge, who had had experience with the Hong Kong plague of 1894, to take what Rand boasted were "the most drastic" measures ever undertaken in India "to stamp out an epidemic." Despite the violent opposition that these stringent measures aroused among the native population, at least some members of the British government, including Rand's eventual successor, W.L. Reade, remained firmly convinced of their efficacy, even though the plague broke out again at the end of July 1897, after only a two-month interval of dormancy.

It is perhaps ironic that just when the first epidemic of plague in Pune had subsided, Rand fell victim to the hand of an unknown assassin on June 22, 1897. We have already seen how native newspapers chronicled the rising tide of resentment that engulfed Rand (see above). From the chairman's point of view, however, he was fully justified in distrusting native agency as unreliable. His "Report on the Poona Plague Operation," submitted just before he died, claimed that native municipal councillors had failed to act boldly enough to halt the plague when it first appeared in the city, and he faulted native "leading men," including some municipal commissioners, for succumbing to panic and choosing to flee rather than stay and combat the disease. He also considered the mass of common people as inclined to resist his measures out of sheer "ignorance," while Hindu religious leaders were liable to "work against any operations that might be set on foot by Government". British soldiers, on the other hand, were regarded by Rand as "disciplined" and "honest," who only needed native volunteers as "interpreters". Rand was left utterly convinced of both the necessity of carrying plague measures through to their conclusion and of doing so without native input. But some of Rand's arguments and complaints had a self-fulfilling quality to them. If native input was so brusquely brushed aside, it is not surprising that so few should volunteer for duty. And if the municipal council had not done enough to combat plague, it also had its efforts blocked or ignored by the government. While Rand's complaint that native community leaders had fled the scene was also voiced by Pune's newspapers, these drew the opposite conclusion – that more "native agency" was required, not less.

By the fall of 1897, Pune's newspapers were celebrating a turnabout in government policy, whereby native input was now welcomed and native volunteers put in charge of house searches. Native volunteers were also put in charge of each of the sixteen wards of the city in order to supervise plague operations, under the direction of an European officer. One of these native volunteers, a municipal commissioner named Vishnu Anant Patwardhan, testified before the Indian Plague Commission, on February 23, 1899, that he wanted modifications of plague measures to go further, to include local ward hospitals and nearby segregation houses so that relatives could easily visit and attend their sick, private disinfection of houses by the owners themselves, immediate inspection of corpses to avoid delays in cremation, and selective implementation of measures to accommodate higher-class natives. The Chief Plague Authority in Pune, W.L. Reade, was resistant to such modifications as home segregation and voluntary evacuation on the grounds that it would risk spreading the disease. This was despite the fact that he was forced to admit that the native volunteer system had resulted in more reliable information about plague and better implementation of plague measures, while measures favored by the authorities, such as corpse inspection, had their limitations. The case of Reade is a fascinating one, as the following two documents illustrate.

■ Letter from Major W.L. Reade to Sir Arthur Godley, March 3, 1898

W.L. Reade, a surgeon-major in the Royal Army Medical Corps, first came to Pune to serve in an advisory capacity to its Plague Committee in February 1897. Prior to that, he had been stationed in Hong Kong at the time of its plague outbreak in 1894, when hospitalization and segregation also had been attempted in order to combat the disease. Since the assassination of W.C. Rand in June 1897, Reade seems to have been in effective charge of plague operations in Pune. Shortly thereafter, on March 3, 1898, Reade, writing from the comfort of the Club of Western India in Pune, addressed a letter to Sir Arthur Godley, head of the India Office in London, in which he purported to present a report on the progress of plague operations in Pune. On May 7, 1898, Pune's Plague Committee was officially dissolved and Reade given command of all plague operations with the title of chief plague authority. Reade was to become one of the highest paid medical officers in the corps, drawing more in pay than the surgeon-general of Bombay.

According to Reade, what were his tactics for eradicating the epidemic, and how well were they working? How did he portray those tactics and their results as being received by the native populace? What did he foresee as the political and cultural consequences of his anti-plague measures? Is there any evidence that suggests Reade might have had ulterior motives for presenting such a report? What might have been those motives?

The Plague here has been practically stamped out and we have had no case for several days. Our organization has been reduced to corpse inspection and 3 superintendents for supervision of census.

Of course, we may expect some imported cases from Bombay, but with our corpse inspection we have no reason to fear, as they can be stamped out at once. We have now one central office, and *all* cases of illness, however slight, have to be reported there. Any corpse that is inspected, the previous illness of which has not been reported, is treated as if it was a plague corpse, the house is disinfected and the inhabitants of the house are sent to the segregation camp and receive

---

Source: British Library, India Office Records, MSS Eur. F.102/6A, fols. 80r–85v.

only half subsistence as a punishment. The consequence is that nearly every case of illness, however slight, is reported.

Of course, we examine into each case and, if it is found to be a genuine case of sudden death, we do not segregate.

The gratitude of the people in the success of the measures is simply unbounded, and Col. Cregh and my time is now largely taken up in attending what are called Pansapori parks, at which speeches are made, and we are garlanded!

I consider that plague operations, properly undertaken, present one of the best opportunities for riveting our rule in India, as it is not only an opportunity for showing a kindness to the people, but also for showing the superiority of our Western Science, and thoroughness. The reports from the Punjab and the . . . [unidentified] territory are by no means encouraging, and I fear the centres of endemic infection are spreading. Of Bombay City you probably know as much as I do officially, but from private sources I hear that chaos reigns. . . .

So far as I have been able to learn, not a place, with the exception of Poona [Pune], have instituted a corpse inspection, and when the [monsoon] rains commence, everything will again be darkness as to the progress of the disease. I would advise that the disease cannot be stamped out of the country until a corpse inspection is established in every large town where the disease has occurred. I have gone to some trouble in finding out from influential natives if the inspection interferes in the least with any caste or religious prejudice, and the answer is quite unanimous that it does not. This quite bears out our experience here, we have never had the slightest difficulty over it, and moreover, all the corpses are examined by a doctor (male), not a single lady doctor is employed. Without wishing to be an alarmist, I should like you at home to face matters as they will be at the commencement of the rains, even supposing the disease has been reduced under epidemic proportions.

You must remember that in the majority of places, it is only scorched and it will burst into flame again under favouring surroundings.

It is during the period of quies[c]ence that our time comes to blow it out or smother it entirely.

Extreme and untiring vigilance will be called for, and the question is, will they be forthcoming?

Will you think me very egotistical [*sic*] and self confident when I say that, given a free hand, I could ensure that there would be no recurrent epidemic of the disease, as it can be stamped out in [its] initial stage, and this without revolting the prejudice of the people.

I feel now that I know every turn and twist that the disease can take and every minutiae of the reformation necessary to combat it.

While I am sure that the India Office have given me every support it was possible to give, I also feel sure you will recognise that this support has been largely inoperative. I don't mention this in an ungracious spirit, as I tap and enter into your difficulties, as I know you will enter into mine.

It is, of course, for the India Office to decide when the period of suggestion should cease, and the time for specific instructions has become necessary. I consider that if I were appointed a temporary member for plague purposes of Lord Sandhurst's Executive Council, that I should have all the powers necessary for dealing with the plague.

This suggestion is made from no wish of an increase in the very handsome pay I luckily draw, my only wish is an increase of usefulness which the appointment would give.

■ Indian Plague Commission, *Minutes of Evidence,* February 24, 1899

Nearly a year after he had written his letter to Sir Arthur Godley in London, W.L. Reade was called to appear before the Indian Plague Commission, which since November 1898 had been holding hearings on various aspects of the plague in India. The hearing was held over the course of two days at the Council Hall in Pune before five examiners and a secretary. The second day of the hearings, on February 24, 1899, was entirely given over to examination of Reade, its "star witness".

See if you can detect any difference in tone or even message between Reade's recorded testimony and his letter to Godley. If such differences exist, to what do you ascribe them? Of the two documents, which seems to give a more accurate picture of reality? Why? To what extent and in what manner, if any, does even the more accurate source seem flawed and incomplete?

Council Hall, Poona, February 24, 1899, Major W.L. Reade called and examined.

Prof. T.R. Fraser, president of the commission: Are you in a position to state briefly what were the measures employed during the first epidemic?

Source: Indian Plague Commission, *Minutes of Evidence*, 4 vols. (London: H.M.S.O., 1900), 3: 160–167.

Major W.L. Reade: Rigorous isolation of all the sick in hospital was carried out, compulsory detention of the contacts in segregation camps, and disinfection of houses and clothes, and there was an organisation of search parties by British soldiers and sepoys accompanied by native workers. . . .

Fraser: Is the rapid decline in the first epidemic, from December 1896 to the end of March or April 1897, coincident with any plague measures that were adopted?

Reade: Undoubtedly.

Fraser: Which plague measures?

Reade: The measures which were brought into force, namely, the isolation of sick into hospital, and the segregation of the contacts. . . .

Fraser: What measures were adopted in the second epidemic?

Reade: In the second epidemic we relied more on the help of the native people, and we gradually lessened the strictness of the measures, and after a time we modified them more. We have done away with the compulsory detention of the contacts in a segregation camp, and we have lessened our measures quite recently with regard to hospital treatment, but I think the chief measure was the lessening of the strictness of our segregation system. We created a system of open segregation by which people were allowed out during the day, and they had to report themselves at night. We had a roll-call every morning. . . .

Fraser: What was the effect of all this modification?

Reade: These measures came into force about a week before the fall, the 27th November is put down as the date of the revised measures, and from the 11th of December [1897] there was a continuous fall [in mortality during the second epidemic]. . . .

Fraser: Putting aside the fall in the mortality, what do you think was the valuable result of this change of organisation that you speak of?

Reade: I think it gave more confidence to the people.

Fraser: In what way?

Reade: That they had someone to apply to.

Fraser: Did it result in your getting better information as to the cases?

Reade: Undoubtedly. . . .

Mr. J.P. Hewett: Do you find any objection on the part of the people here to corpse inspection?

Reade: No, none.

Hewett: If you have any specific instance, perhaps you will tell us?

Reade: The only specific instance brought to my notice was with regard to the inspection of the corpse of a fakir [Muslim holy man]. It was brought to our notice by one of the Chief Volunteers of a Pet [ward] who said that the man was of holy habits and an ascetic, and that the people did not wish his corpse to be handled by an European doctor. We assented, and said that they might have a Brahman doctor, the European doctor being present. There was no difficulty about it. There was also one objection from a Muhammadan, but that was easily got over. The corpse was allowed to be inspected. . . .

Mr. A. Cumine: You have only had two or three objections made to the examination of corpses, but have you had any complaints, from people saying that corpses have lain for a very long time in their houses because the medical officer has not come to examine them?

Reade: Yes.

Cumine: How many such cases, roughly, have you had?

Reade: I have certainly had two or three complaints. In the volunteer meetings that have been held that point has come up for discussion. There have undoubtedly been two or three complaints made in that way, but very few written ones.

Cumine: There have been undoubtedly complaints of what?

Reade: That a delay has occurred. . . .

Prof. A.E. Wright: In view of the fact that a large number of cases can only be classified as "suspicious" and in view of the fact that you cannot in these cases arrive at a definite opinion as to whether you are or are not dealing with plague, do you not think that corpse inspection, as at present carried out, is unsatisfactory?

Reade: No, I do not think it is.

Wright: I presume you can never, by your present methods, certify the town to be free from plague?

Reade: I think you may arrive at it by bacteriological examination.

Wright: Do you think that corpse inspection ought to be supplemented by bacteriological examination of the suspicious corpses?

Reade: Yes.

Wright: Have you any means of supplementing your corpse inspection by bacteriological examination?

Reade: No, not in Poona. . . .

Pneumonic Plague in Harbin, Manchuria

With 10 to 15 people a day dying of pneumonic plague at the beginning of December 1910 in Harbin, a city of a little over 70,000 inhabitants that served as the main shipping and transportation hub of China's largest province, Manchuria, the Chinese imperial government decided that something had to be done. It responded by sending one of its leading doctors, Wu Liande, to assess the situation. Dr. Wu, who received his medical degree at the University of Cambridge in England, was convinced that only drastic measures along the lines of what the British had done in India would stem the crisis. In addition to his English education and training, Dr. Wu was perhaps equally motivated to favor a Western medical approach by his embarrassment at the incompetence of Chinese officials at Harbin, who included an opium addict, and rivalry with Russian doctors, who treated the sizable Russian population in the city. Wu accordingly recommended such measures as halting of railway traffic, house-to-house inspection, setting up detention camps and isolation hospitals, and disinfection or destruction of the homes of plague patients. Because pneumonic plague is highly infectious, Dr. Wu also introduced the wearing of cotton-gauze masks. In addition, he advocated the cremation of 2,000 plague corpses that had accumulated on the streets of Harbin by the end of January, which apparently had contributed more to the psychological demoralization of the populace and medical staff than had posed a serious health threat. This request seems to have encountered some opposition from government officials, for it was not approved until Wu had explained its necessity to the imperial court. When the grisly bonfire was started on the Chinese New Year, January 31, 1911, it must have presented a truly horrifying spectacle as hundreds of bodies were set on fire using wood and kerosene and continued to burn for two whole days (see Figure 3.2). Yet Dr. Wu reports that the removal of the plague dead from peoples' sight "was in the eyes of the public a greater and more glorious achievement than all our other anti-plague efforts combined."

The plague outbreak of 1910–1911 had caught the Chinese government, which at the time was ineffective and tottering toward imminent collapse, largely unawares and ill-prepared to fight pneumonic plague. Even after the disease appeared in Manchuria, it was several months before the Foreign Office dispatched Dr. Wu, by which time the disease had reached epidemic proportions in Harbin. The doctor received his instructions on December 10, 1910 but only arrived on the scene on December 24, and by that time the plague had already killed hundreds. Compared to the Russian side of the town, which Wu described as a "miniature Moscow," the Chinese quarter was overcrowded and dirty, consisting of "narrow streets" and

FIGURE 3.2 *Plague Victims.* Heaps of pneumonic plague victims and kindling await cremation in a pit in Harbin, Manchuria in 1911. According to Wu Liande, these bodies were cremated more to boost morale than for hygienic reasons.

"uninviting mud-and-straw huts" which, we have seen from the experience of India, was conducive to the spread of plague. Detention camps for those who had come into contact with plague patients had to be improvised at Harbin out of railway boxcars that were lying empty due to the halt of traffic during the plague, while in other cities, camps were hurriedly erected out of corrugated iron. The hospitals that existed to treat plague patients were evidently unable to prevent them from being re-infected by new admissions, indicating that isolation wards were simply unavailable. Nor did the Manchu government have the political clout to enforce all the measures recommended by Dr. Wu. It was unable, for example, to completely halt the fur trade in tarabagan skins, which was considered essential to prevent the outbreak of another epidemic. Because the Chinese Revolution broke out in October 1911, the government did not complete construction of its first plague hospital at Harbin until September of 1912, following the abdication on February 12, 1912 of the last emperor of China, when the 268-year-old Manchu, or Qing, Dynasty was replaced by the Republic of China.

Regardless of the obstacles confronting them, Dr. Wu and his colleagues at Harbin succeeded in stemming the tide of plague by early 1911. Moreover, despite the new government's instability and Japanese entrenchment in southern Manchuria, by the end of 1912, five hospitals had been built at strategic locations throughout Manchuria – Harbin, Sansing, Taheiho, Lahasusu, and Manchouli. The main hospital at Harbin was able to accommodate 300 patients, divided into separate wards for plague patients, contacts, and suspects, and it contained a bacteriological laboratory, disinfection station, museum, library, and operating theater. Further, as the result of an international plague conference held at Mukden in April 1911, when pneumonic plague had finally abated in Manchuria, the Chinese government was persuaded to start a Plague Prevention Service for North Manchuria with the mission to conduct research into pneumonic plague and to prevent or stamp out its appearance in the province. With Wu Liande as director and chief medical officer, the Service performed a function similar to that of the Indian Plague Commission, churning out an impressive production of articles and books, the vast majority by Wu himself, that explored in great detail various clinical and epidemiological aspects of pneumonic plague.

When an epidemic of pneumonic plague broke out again in Manchuria in 1920–1921, the government found itself better prepared to face the crisis, despite the chaotic political situation of a country immersed in a time of troubles known as the Warlord Period. An outbreak of pneumonic plague in Harbin in January 1921 was met by housing all confirmed and suspect plague patients in the city's new hospital, although contacts were still isolated in railway boxcars. House-to-house inspection (with particular attention paid to coolie inns), disinfection, and cremation of plague corpses were also carried out. In addition, railway traffic was restricted and theaters and brothels were closed. The quality of the sanitary staff, particularly the disinfecting and burial squads, was also much improved, as compared to the first outbreak, when such teams had to be hurriedly cobbled together out of alcoholics and "morally unfit" persons. As Wu boasted, the results could be seen in the fact that mortality was significantly down from the previous epidemic. Yet there was still opposition from some sectors of the populace, and there continued to occur the concealment of plague

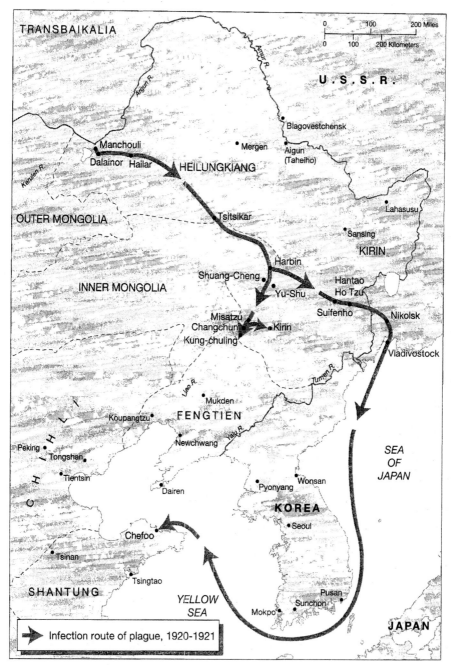

MAP 3.1   Centers of pneumonic plague in Manchuria.

cases, for fear of hospitalization, isolation, and disinfection. As in India, plague rumors circulated, and distrust of the government's hospital was also demonstrated by the fact that practitioners of traditional medicine briefly opened a plague house. On occasion, opposition to the Service turned violent. In addition to the examples cited by Wu in his *Report* (see below), he "received many threatening and abusive letters." The authors of the *Report* were also well aware that similar resistance had been encountered by the "doctors and sanitary attendants" who had attempted to contain bubonic plague in India.

But if the Chinese realized they were repeating history, they seem to have learned none of its lessons. There is little evidence that Dr. Wu and his colleagues were willing to accommodate native customs and traditions or to moderate their measures in response to public opinion, as the British had felt compelled to do in India. Wu was frankly dismissive of native practitioners "of the old school" in Manchuria. At best, these "quacks" were, in his eyes, a topic for amusing anecdotes, and at worst, they drained much-needed funds from the Service and hindered its work. He also did not seem to have much patience for the peasant "coolies" and commoners of China. Like practitioners of traditional medicine, the best that could be said about them was that they offered only passive resistance to modern plague measures, and they suffered in comparison with their foreign counterparts in Manchuria – Russians, who were able to afford better hygiene such as water-closets, and Japanese, who had the benefits of universal education which overcame their fear of plague measures.

Yet in defense of the uncompromising measures taken by Dr. Wu and his colleagues and their apparent blindness to the lessons of India, it should be remembered that, from the Service's standpoint, it was fighting a highly contagious, deadly disease, but one that, in the words of Dr. Wu, was one of the "few infectious diseases" that could be "easily controlled." At the close of his *Treatise on Pneumonic Plague,* which reflected over a decade of experience fighting the disease, Dr. Wu predicted the eradication of both pneumonic and bubonic plague as part of the "general progress of the human race," even though others observed "that the malady is more rampant now than in the past." For Wu Liande, the steadily expanding modern "knowledge of science and sanitation" would enable "mankind to protect itself against an invasion [of disease] with far greater ease than was formerly the case," a fairly confident boast given that no proven vaccine or serum cure had yet been found for plague. In fact, the ease with which it was claimed that pneumonic plague could be controlled may have led Wu to conclude, as he did, that the medieval Black Death, a subject in which he took a keen interest, was not plague but influenza, a disease that had recently erupted into a worldwide pandemic in 1918–1919.[7]

Reading Wu's description of measures taken at Harbin to combat pneumonic plague, while obviously designed to impress with their demonstration of progressive techniques of medicine and sanitation, can, nonetheless, be a chilling experience. He ruled out home segregation of contacts, as was tried in several towns in India, on the grounds that it allowed for insufficient monitoring of potential cases, although he was willing to make exceptions in the case of evacuation. While such a policy may appear cruel "to the uninitiated," since seemingly healthy persons were evicted from their homes, individual interests, Wu urged, "must to a certain degree be sacrificed for those of the community," an argument, however, that had not washed among many of the natives of India. Sick-rooms in the Harbin plague hospital were deliberately designed to be "puritanlike," with little more than a bed and cast-iron spittoon for the coughing up of sputum, an arrangement that probably made them hardly more hospitable than the railway box-cars used for isolating contacts. Nor can the appearance of hospital staff, who during the 1920–1921 epidemic were decked out not only with a mask but also with goggles, hood, rubber gloves and boots, and an apron, have been very inviting or comforting. The fact that barbed-wire fences and police guards, who were issued orders to shoot on sight any escapees, were used to separate wards can only add to the overall impression that here was a prison camp for the condemned, rather than a place for healing.

In the end, however, not even the most well-intentioned, compassionate, and courageous of medical staff can impose such draconian and unappealing measures without some degree of cooperation from the victims. Dr. Wu noted the philosophical resignation of his fellow countrymen which allowed him to carry out the drastic expedient of mass cremation, even though the Chinese have an "abhorrence" for this method of disposal in "ordinary times." Despite his Western-bred contempt for masses ignorant of modern sanitation and science, he paid homage to the voluntary efforts – albeit guided by "enlightened officials" – of populations at plague control, which included even the sacrificial entombment of whole families afflicted by the plague in their houses. This seems to militate against his pessimistic conclusion that "affected people are rarely willing to co-operate with the authorities in carrying out the plans devised for their safety." His colleague, Dr. Chun, was perhaps more generous in paying tribute to the "remarkable fortitude" of the Chinese laborers who came into the hospital as plague victims:

> He is the best patient in the world and is a staunch fatalist. He will suffer and say nothing. He sees his comrades die and utters not a murmur, fully knowing that he himself would soon share the same fate. Moreover, he is very grateful and appreciates what little one can do for him. He is polite and obliging under all circumstances. In all these respects, he is entitled to one's admiration and deep respect.[8]

Howsoever much these medical men preferred to attribute their victories over plague to "modern-trained physicians and their methods," they had to admit, if even grudgingly, that only the acquiescence of their patients made them possible.

■ Wu Liande, *North Manchurian Plague Prevention Service Reports, 1918–1922*

The North Manchurian Plague Prevention Service, headed by the Cambridge-trained physician, Wu Liande, was established on October 1, 1912, in response to the extraordinary mortality of the pneumonic plague outbreak throughout Manchuria in the winter of 1910–1911, which killed an estimated 60,000 inhabitants. A second outbreak occurred in Manchuria during the winter of 1920–1921; this time, a total of just 8,500 victims were carried off by the epidemic. Credit for the lower death rate was claimed by the Prevention Service, which established a network of hospitals in Manchuria, including one at Harbin, which opened on December 16, 1912. During the second epidemic of 1920–1921, the Harbin hospital served as a center from which the Chinese government strove to combat the disease. The Plague Prevention Service also sponsored extensive research into all aspects of pneumonic plague, which were published in three *Reports*, beginning in 1914 and ending in 1922. The following excerpt is from Dr. Wu's third *Report*, which chronicles measures undertaken at Harbin to fight the epidemic of 1920–1921.

This report also records the various responses of the Chinese population of Harbin to the efforts of Dr. Wu and his staff. What were those efforts? What were the responses? How did Dr. Wu attempt to counter opposition to his efforts? To what factors did Dr. Wu ascribe the Service's success in suppressing the epidemic? By what statistical measure did he claim vindication for his anti-plague measures? Were Dr. Wu and his staff able to cure any victims of the plague? Finally, Dr. Wu provides a series of anecdotes that put a human face on the epidemic. What do these stories suggest about the obstacles that members of the Service faced and the ways in which they were able to overcome them?

As in the previous epidemic of 1910–11, Harbin was the headquarters of the anti-plague organisation, from which all instructions and reports were sent. . . .

The Chinese city health work is still in the hands of untrained police officers, who only seek expert advice when a serious epidemic like plague threatens. Fortunately, the plague Prevention Service, with its largest hospital and principal laboratory situated in Harbin, has established a wide reputation throughout China, and by its successful control of epidemic and other diseases in the past has won the confidence of officials and merchants alike. When plague broke out in 1921, the ignorant classes were only half convinced, but they showed no open hostility. The real opposition came from the unruly soldiers, but even the hearts of these men were touched when they saw the tenderness and fearlessness with which Chinese doctors and nurses attended their friends in this most dangerous of all diseases. . . .

The first plague case in Harbin was recorded on Jan. 22 [1921], when an ex-miner died suddenly in a house near the hospital after having arrived from Dalainor the previous day. Among four contacts (mother, sister, sister-in-law and male friend) who were admitted into our Hospital, only the sister-in-law took the disease on 26th and died the next day. This patient had fever, fast pulse and tightness in chest the first day, developed cough, later on spat blood, and died in the evening. Her sputum and blood showed the plague bacilli in large numbers.

Source: North Manchurian Plague Prevention Service Reports (1918–1922), ed. Wu Lien Teh (Tientsin: Tientsin Press, Ltd., 1922), 13–22.

In a small village four miles from the Chinese city [within Harbin] another miner from Dalainor died of plague on Jan. 26. Three men living in the same room with him also died, and in addition members of three neighbouring families, with the result that in this small village of 73 huts and 400 souls, eleven persons died of plague between Jan. 26 and Feb. 6. Fortunately owing to the early precautions taken at Harbin, all cases found were at once admitted into hospital, while the contacts were received in [railway] box-cars, each holding the members of one household (average six). It was evident that a trying time lay in front of us, and the whole efforts of the Service were concentrated upon limiting the outbreak to the smallest possible proportion. . . . The plague wards could accomodate 60 sick [*sic*], while the suspect wards had 50 beds. It was found that plague patients rarely survived beyond the second day after admission, as they were killed off so quickly. . . .

All suspects and plague cases were sent to our Hospital in Fuchiatien [district], the few Russian sick (eight) being cared for in the Municipal Hospital. The Chinese city was divided into 5 districts, each with its corps of Police, dressers, inspectors, sanitary attendants, and disinfection squads. Patients were at once removed to hospital, while suspected corpses or dead found in the streets received spleen punctures [as blood sample]. . . . All cadavers found in the streets were sent to the common cremation pit to be burnt. Well-to-do and educated persons were sometimes thrown into the streets unclaimed, because the relatives after hiding them during sickness were afraid to report after death for fear of being isolated in the wagons. One of the most difficult problems of plague-prevention in China was this passive opposition of the populace in not reporting cases when alive and then throwing the bodies out when dead. If there had been co-operation between the public and the authorities at the beginning, the epidemic would have been more confined, but the cases were hidden and the families or friends were thus infected. This fear of isolation is prevalent in North and South China alike, and used to be the same in Japan until the new universal education of the masses produced its beneficial results. The dead in the plague-hospital, numbering 1312, were all cremated in two pits dug within its precincts. Each pit measured 12 by 12 by 10 feet deep. Large pieces of firewood were laid at the bottom, some bodies uncoffined were thrown in, then more wood, and so on. The fire was started by pouring two gallons of kerosene on the pile, and then lighting. The masses burnt fiercely in the open, because of the confined space, and even on cold windy days no difference was observed. In this way 80 to 100 bodies could be economically cremated every day with slight attention from two attendants. The fatty constituents of the cadavers helped to keep up the fire once it was lit, and at the end of the day only white crumbled bones were left as residue. . . .

Because of the large percentage of deaths it was not surprising that rumours began to spread that we *took in* patients but did *not let them out*, and something uncanny must therefore have happened within the hospital compounds. Stories were current that our staff poisoned wells, flour and food in order to obtain a reward of $3 for each dead. My bulletin of March 13th contained the following:

> The past week has been a very anxious one for our anti-plague staff for the concentrated suspicion of and prejudice against our policy of removal of the sick to hospital, isolation of contacts, systematic inspection of inns and other sources of infection, closing of theatres, low brothels, etc., coupled with the restriction of railway traffic a[n]d our inability to cure the plague victims resulted in numerous rumours to discredit our dangerous and humane mission and in some instances to actual threats of physical violence to our members. For instance, the Chief Medical Officer* was accused of shooting the sick in the plague compound and was threatened with a similar fate should an opportunity offer itself, our house-to-house inspection doctors were on several occasions faced with revolvers and knives in the course of their duty, while the sanitary assistants were almost obliged to swallow some of the disinfectants used in the disinfected houses.
>
> At Asheho a mob of sixty visited the isolation station, set free the two contacts confined there and chased the doctor in charge. It speaks well for the discipline of our staff that in the presence of so much provocation and the loss by plague of one of their leaders they have stuck to their duty and not resigned *en masse*.

To counteract these evil influences, we issued thousands of circulars, published a daily newspaper containing particulars about the sick and dead, reports from other infected localities, articles dealing with plague and health matters, etc. Our assistants also gave public lectures whenever possible and answered any questions that might be asked them by their audience. In fact our staff were faced with open attack from resentful and frightened persons as well as unseen danger from the plague germ. But all stuck to their duties with a cheerful heart. The masses refused to take sanitary precautions and yet expected to escape infection. But the time came when our efforts were bound to succeed,

*Dr. Wu himself.

the mortality curve showed a steady decline from April 10th [1921] and finally reached zero point on May 15th. The Harbin epidemic thus lasted nearly four months and claimed 3125 deaths out of a population of 300,000, as compared with over 7,000 out of a population of 70,000 in the previous outbreak (1910–1911). The death list might have been 30,000 or ten times greater if energetic measures had not been taken from the beginning. As it was, the epidemic was prevented from seriously invading the populous towns of South Manchuria and North China, less than 400 dying from plague in these latter regions as compared with 35,000 in 1910–1911. . . .

A few interesting, sometimes humorous, episodes may now be related in connection with our anti-plague experience:

> Some of the most noisy detractors of our work were the native quacks who persisted in beguiling the public as to their ability to cure the disease. When patients came with fever and cough, they always gave hopeful prescriptions. If the sickness was not infectious, the patient got well and the quack's reputation jumped skywards; should it turn out to be true plague, both patient and quack often died. In Harbin alone, we recorded seven deaths among the old-style practitioners; one was the 'vice-president of the medical research society' whose body was thrown out into the street by his wife in order to escape isolation of the family. At Dalainor one quack after catching the disease passed it on to his wife and all four children. None survived. . . .
>
> The Inspection parties sometimes made mistakes. One man was sent in from the city because he had a fast pulse and had spat up something red. At hospital, we learnt that he had been eating crab apples and the red spit was due to them. Needless to say, the man went home delighted.
>
> Most coolies were credulous and intensely ignorant about matters hygienic, but Dr. Chun (our Senior Med. Officer) got into conversation on April 9 with a Chinese carriage driver on his way home. The driver was young and pleasant and informed the doctor that on the previous day he was driving a fare when a policeman suddenly stopped his carriage and demanded where he was driving a *corpse* to. His live fare of fifteen minutes before had died of plague while in the carriage! The driver also said that he did not believe the rumours about doctors poisoning wells, food, etc., for he knew from experience that they were kind-hearted and treated all the poor well. . . .
>
> Many Chinese firmly believed in the efficacy of opium in keeping off plague, so much so that non-smokers were induced to try

it during the epidemic. At Dalainor, a Japanese woman openly maintained an opium smoking and morphine establishment. Her business was most prosperous at the height of the epidemic. One day three plague corpses were found in her opium den. That served as an excellent reason for closing altogether her nefarious business, which at ordinary times might have required the cooperation of her consul.

NOTES

1. Samuel K. Cohn, Jr., "The Black Death: End of a Paradigm," *The American Historical Review* 107 (2002): 703–738; idem, *The Black Death Transformed: Disease and Culture in Early Renaissance Europe* (London and Oxford: Arnold and Oxford University Press, 2002), esp. 7–40.
2. David Arnold, *Colonizing the Body: State Medicine and Epidemic Disease in Nineteenth-Century India* (Berkeley and Los Angeles: University of California Press, 1993), 238.
3. Ibid., 211.
4. Indian Plague Commission, *Minutes of Evidence* and *Report*, 5 vols. (London: H.M.S.O., 1900–1901), 3: 292.
5. *North Manchurian Plague Prevention Service Reports (1918–1922)*, ed. Wu Lien-Teh (Tientsin: Tientsin Press, Ltd., 1922), 132; Wu Lien-Teh, *A Treatise on Pneumonic Plague* (Geneva: Publications of the League of Nations, 1926), 9.
6. *North Manchurian Plague Prevention Service Reports (1911–1913)*, ed. Wu Lien-Teh (Cambridge: Cambridge University Press, 1914), 20–21.
7. Wellcome Library, WA/HMM/CO/Chr/A/120, Box 89.
8. *North Manchurian Plague Prevention Service Reports (1918–1922)*, 171–172.

CHAPTER

4

A Modern Plague: AIDS in Sub-Saharan Africa, 1982 to the Present

THE AIDS VICTIMS OF SUB-SAHARAN AFRICA

The disease known as acquired immunodeficiency syndrome (AIDS) is easily the most severe crisis to hit the African continent in modern times, and perhaps in all of its history. There are any number of statistics one can cite in support of this statement. As of 2005, sub-Saharan Africa was home to 25.8 million people infected with the human immunodeficiency virus (HIV) that causes AIDS, which represents 60–70 percent of all those worldwide living with the disease, even though this region harbors just over 10 percent of the world's population. While the percentage of the population infected across the sub-Saharan continent is under 10 percent, in some countries the percentage is so high – roughly a quarter of the population infected in Zimbabwe, Lesotho, and South Africa, and, astonishingly, nearly 40 percent infected in Botswana and Swaziland – that the epidemic is virtually guaranteed a self-perpetuating focus of infection for the foreseeable future. That more than 17 million Africans have died of AIDS since the start of the epidemic in the early 1980s means that half a dozen countries, almost all in the southern part of Africa, are now experiencing zero, or even negative, population growth and life expectancies of under 40 years of age from birth, which are expected to drop even further to around 30 years of age by 2010. AIDS is now the leading cause of death in sub-Saharan Africa, with a yearly average death rate of over 2 million, killing twice as many as the second leading cause of death and ten times more deadly than war. Moreover, Africa is a bellwether for future epicenters of the epidemic that are expected to emerge in India and China by 2020: together, these two countries account for nearly half the world's population and may be home to as many as 15 million HIV-infected persons.

THE DISEASE'S CHARACTERISTICS

AIDS is a new disease never seen before, or at least recognized, in the history of humankind. Although caused by a virus, AIDS is produced by a rather unique family of organisms called retroviruses, which were discovered in animals only in the 1970s and in humans in 1980. Instead of DNA, retroviruses have as the core of their genetic material RNA (ribonucleic acid), along with enzymes, such as reverse transcriptase, which give it the ability to reproduce the host cell's DNA and thus make itself genetically indistinguishable from other host cells. Retroviruses are characterized by their ability to replicate very rapidly (each virus has a life cycle of only one and a half days) and hence mutate in response to new environmental conditions, and they tend to be latent, or lie dormant, inside cells until "triggered" into replicating activity. These characteristics make it very difficult for the body's immune system to target and destroy invading retroviruses. Furthermore, the HIV that causes AIDS, part of a subgroup of retroviruses known as the lentivirus, specifically targets the cells that make up the human body's immune defense system, namely the CD4 cells that organize and execute the body's immune response to infections. Ironically, then, HIV attacks the very cells upon which the body relies to fight disease. HIV is therefore a particularly insidious kind of disease organism.

Since HIV attacks the immune system, it does not so much cause a specific disease as cause an immune suppression, which makes the body vulnerable to other organisms that inevitably will result in death. These "opportunistic infections" most commonly include tuberculosis, pneumonia, and cerebral toxoplasmosis among terminal AIDS patients in Africa. In addition, the World Health Organization (WHO) includes Kaposi's sarcoma and cryptococcal meningitis as defining diseases in its case definition of an African AIDS diagnosis, or, in the absence of these conditions, telltale symptoms such as severe weight loss ("slim disease"), diarrhea, persistent cough, and oral candidiasis (such as thrush). Without antiretroviral treatment, an AIDS patient will typically live for 8–10 years before the onset of the opportunistic infection that will lead to his or her death, although the incubation period may be even shorter in the developing world due to poor nutrition, lack of access to good health care, and an intensive infectious-disease environment.

There is today no cure for AIDS, and the scientific consensus seems to be that there most likely will never be one, given HIV's ability to insinuate itself into the DNA of host cells and thus lie dormant and impervious to viral antibodies. Then, when HIV is activated, its ability to rapidly replicate, and thus mutate, makes it an extremely challenging organism to target and eliminate. Currently, there are at least nine different subtypes, labeled A through K, of the main M group of HIV-1 viruses that cause over 99 percent of HIV infections around the world. The other groups, or strains, of HIV-1, N and O, are confined to Cameroon and to other West and Central African countries. In addition, at least seven circulating recombinant forms (CRF) of HIV-1, which involve combinations of two or more of the A–K subtypes, have been identified from Africa. A second human immunodeficiency virus, labeled HIV-2, was discovered in 1985 and was found to be more genetically similar to a simian immunodeficiency virus (SIV) in mangabey and macaque monkeys than to HIV-1. HIV-2, largely prevalent in West Africa, is less transmissible and virulent and has a slower progression to full-blown AIDS than HIV-1, even though it also targets CD4 immune cells and is likewise transmitted through blood and semen. HIV-2 also seems to be less mutative, currently present in only two subtypes, A and B. The genetic diversity of HIV is both regional and individual. For example, the B subtype of HIV-1 is responsible for most infections in the United States and Europe, whereas the A, C, and D subtypes are especially prevalent in Africa. But even within a single AIDS patient, genetic variations of HIV can occur.

SEARCH FOR A VACCINE AND EFFECTIVE THERAPIES

Since a cure for AIDS is unlikely, research efforts have focused on finding a vaccine and on developing antiretroviral therapies that can slow the progress and transmission of the disease. To date, an effective vaccine for AIDS has not been found, but trials are underway or are planned for a variety of protein, poxvirus, and DNA vaccines that might stimulate antibodies or an immune response to HIV. The difficulties involved include manufacturing a vaccine that can respond to the many subtypes of HIV-1, can be long-lasting, cost-effective, and safe to use. Closely tied up with vaccine development are ethical issues on using Africans as "guinea pigs" for vaccine trials: Is it ethical to test a vaccine on a population that most likely will be unable to afford it, to use placebos on a control group in the face of a life-threatening disease, and to abandon protocols, such as advising subjects on how to avoid the disease, in order to ensure maximum exposure? The other, more successful, area of AIDS research has been in developing antiretroviral therapies (ART), which aim to block and inhibit HIV's entry and replication inside the cell. Because of HIV's ability to mutate, most therapies have now evolved into a multi-drug arsenal that includes a combination of reverse transcriptase inhibitors, such as the drug Zidovudine (AZT), and a protease inhibitor, which targets another enzyme in HIV. In countries where these drugs can be afforded, such as the United States and Europe, they have been proven successful in dramatically prolonging the lives of patients and returning them to a seemingly healthy lifestyle. The downside is that, due to their very success, ARTs seem to have lulled some AIDS patients into a false sense of security to the point that they resume risky behaviors that help spread the virus, despite their reduced viral load, and/or abandon their complex drug regimen, which can lead to resistant strains.

THE ORIGIN OF AIDS

There has been much speculation and controversy concerning the origin of HIV and AIDS. This is not simply an academic debate, because knowing how a disease was born can help elucidate how it can be laid to rest. The scientific consensus seems to be that AIDS originated in Africa and was transmitted from an animal host, namely primates, to humans sometime in the twentieth century. Evidence for this largely comes from a genetic comparison of SIV and HIV: the SIV isolated from macaque and sooty managbey monkeys from West Africa is virtually indistinguishable from HIV-2, while the SIV from chimpanzees is closely related to HIV-1. Since some primates seem to be biologically immune to AIDS, the fact that the viruses in the two species are so similar could be a potent weapon in the development of a vaccine or cure. Additionally, Africa possesses the most genetic diversity in the HIV virus, indicative of an early origin, and the oldest HIV-positive blood result in a human patient has been found in a frozen sample from Zaire dating to 1959. Explaining the crossover of the virus from primates to humans in Africa is perhaps even more fraught with controversy, but various theories have been put forward, including infection of hunters while slaughtering wild monkeys for bush meat, the use of chimpanzee kidneys to culture a polio vaccine during a vaccination campaign in Central Africa in the 1950s, and the injection of monkey blood into the genitals, thighs, and back during ritualistic sexual practices among the Idjwi tribe on Lake Kivu in Central Africa, observed by a French anthropologist during the 1970s. Those who dispute an African origin for AIDS counter that the theory is motivated by vestiges of racist colonialism; that HIV has perhaps been around for centuries, if not millennia; that equally old case histories of opportunistic infections such as Kaposi's sarcoma can be found in other countries besides Africa; and that the current AIDS epidemic emerged simultaneously in North America and Africa in the early 1980s. But both sides would probably agree that to curtail further investigation for fear of laying blame would be more tragic than any perceived stigma attached to the origin of AIDS.

DISEASE TRANSMISSION

The issue of AIDS' origins aside, explaining the biological process of how it is transmitted and spread is straightforward and easy. The HIV virus can only be transmitted through contaminated bodily fluids, namely blood or blood plasma, semen, vaginal excretions, and breast milk; although the virus may be present in saliva and tears in trace amounts, this is not an effective means of transmission. This means that there are limited routes of entry of the virus into the body: sexual intercourse, blood or plasma transfusions, use of contaminated needles or injection devices, open wound infection, and mother-to-child transmission before or after birth. Of these methods, blood transfusion is by far the most efficient mode of transmission, with a 90 percent infection rate. Mother-to-child transmission through intrauterine, intrapartum, and postpartum exposure is the next most contagious mode, with a 30–35 percent infection rate. There is apparently a 0.3 percent risk of infection to health care workers through needlestick injury (or 3 out a 1,000 contaminated needlesticks result in HIV infection), while unsafe injections account for 2 percent of new infections worldwide every year. In the case of unprotected heterosexual intercourse, males run the risk of contracting HIV at a rate of 0.33–1 per 1,000 exposures, while females will be infected 1–2 times per 1,000 exposures. Anal intercourse carries an infection rate of 5–30 per 1,000 exposures. The geographical distribution of these transmission modes also varies. Sub-Saharan Africa, classified as a Pattern I region, is characterized by a predominately heterosexual mode of transmission that historically had an even number of males and females infected, although in recent years higher female infection rates seem to be tilting the ratio to where 1.3 women are infected for every man, with the ratio even higher, at 3.6 to 1, among young people aged 15 to 24. But mother-to-child transmission plays an overwhelming role in infant and child infections, nor can infected needles be discounted as a factor in a region that has limited access to good health facilities. The high prevalence of other sexually transmitted diseases, such as syphilis, gonorrhea, and herpes, and the apparent greater virulence of African HIV subtypes are also important factors in sub-Saharan Africa's high and still growing infection rates. By contrast, Pattern II countries, which include the United States and Western Europe, see transmission of HIV accomplished primarily by homosexual intercourse and intravenous drug use, and have historically seen stabilized or declining infection rates among a predominantly male population, although infections may now be on the rise again due to longer survival rates and abandonment of and fatigue with safe behaviors. Worldwide, 75–85 percent of all HIV infections can be accounted for by sexual transmission.

AIDS AS A SOCIAL CONSTRUCT

The point at which AIDS is transformed from a biological into a social and cultural construct occurs when one begins to discuss the behavioral risk factors that facilitate transmission. These are issues that are also very much tied up with strategies for the prevention of and halt or reversal in the spread of AIDS. For Africa, most of these risk factors revolve around heterosexual intercourse. Those factors thought to increase the risk of contracting the disease include prostitution and commercial sex exchange, migrant work patterns, sexual promiscuity, polygamy, rape and coercive sex, sexual predatoriness (the "sugar daddy" syndrome), widow inheritance, female circumcision, and invasive sexual practices, such as vaginal "dry sex"; male circumcision and condom use, on the other hand, are believed to decrease the risk of contracting HIV. For the most part, risk behaviors are voluntary in nature and imply that they can and should be changed in order to achieve lower HIV infection rates and incidence of AIDS. Some factors, such as prostitution, sexual promiscuity and rape, condom use, and male circumcision, are concerns throughout the world, although some may argue that the incidence of these factors, such as sexual promiscuity – often expressed as that sub-Saharan Africans exhibit a "sex positive" culture – are higher on the African continent. Others seem to be unique to Africa. For example, among numerous tribal cultures in Uganda, Mali, Sierra Leone, Zimbabwe, Zambia, Namibia, Kenya, and Rwanda there exists the tradition of widow inheritance, that is, the widow remarries one of her dead husband's relatives, a custom conducive to the spread of AIDS among the widow's in-laws. It is even reported that some tribal groups, such as the Banyankole people of the Rakai district of Uganda, practice a sexual "cleansing ritual," in which the widow or widower is obligated by tradition to have intercourse with a member of the deceased's family, such as the dead husband's brother. Another prevalent practice attributed to sub-Saharan Africa is that older men, or "sugar daddies," entice adolescent girls into sexual relationships or marriage in the belief that sex with a virgin can cure AIDS. Dry sex – in which herbs, sponges, and desiccating agents are inserted into the vagina in order to tighten the orifice and increase male sexual pleasure – and female circumcision and infibulation – involving the excision or occlusion of the clitoris and other vaginal membranes that is practiced in Muslim communities in the Sudan, Ethiopia, Somalia, and Nigeria – are also closely associated with African culture. Needless to say, such practices result in severe trauma to the vaginal membranes and greatly increase the likelihood of HIV transmission. Those who would attribute Africa's AIDS crisis to voluntary, and therefore readily preventable, risk factors can point to those countries, such as Uganda, Senegal, and Zimbabwe, that have managed to halt or even reverse HIV infection rates largely through effecting a change in sexual behaviors, such as the discouragement of multiple sex partners and the promotion of condom use. Uganda's "success story" is treated in more detail in our first source, an address by President Yoweri Museveni.

The other side of the coin is that Africa's risk behaviors are also determined by historical, socio-economic, cultural, legal, and political forces largely beyond the control of any one individual. To take one of the most contentious examples, the category of commercial sex workers – a nearly all-female category in Africa – comprises a

FIGURE 4.1 AIDS Poster. A poster distributed by the AIDS Prevention Programme in Johannesburg, South Africa, which urges women to unite in order to stop the spread of AIDS.

FIGURE 4.2 AIDS Graveyard. A mass graveyard being excavated in order to accommodate AIDS victims in Namibia. As of 2003, 16,000 Namibians have died of AIDS, while 210,000, out of a total population of nearly 2 million, are currently living with the disease.

wide array of possible members, ranging from professional prostitutes, who entertain several clients a day, to occasional "amateurs," sometimes known in French African countries as *femmes libres*, who enter into long-term relationships with a select group of partners. Their motives are equally varied, but in many instances their engagement in multi-partner sexual intercourse is dictated by dire financial necessity. Particularly in families where the main income earner (usually male) is sick or dies of AIDS, the combination of cost of medical care, funeral costs, and loss of income and inheritance can be catastrophic. For female survivors whose employment options are limited and not as lucrative as men's, their engagement in commercial sex work is all too often a "survival strategy," but one that tragically becomes a "death strategy" when their increased exposure to HIV leads to AIDS. Condom use is also severely limited in a patriarchal society where women generally lack the autonomy to negotiate safe sex practices and where unprotected sex is seen as a sign of trust. Even when one partner is monogamous and faithful, she may therefore be infected through no fault of her own by her spouse's risk behaviors, particularly in situations where the income earner must travel and be absent for long periods in order to find work. According to one study, "it is estimated that 60–80 percent of African women with HIV have had only one partner but were infected because they were not in a position to negotiate safe sex or prevent their partners from having additional sexual contacts."[1] Colonialism also has left a legacy of migrant labor, whether this be the mine workers of South Africa or the Chagga people of Mount Kilimanjaro who work the coffee plantations of Tanzania, which separate families for long stretches at a time. This naturally lends itself to partner exchange among isolated husbands and wives, or what the French Africans call their *deuxième bureau* and even *troisième bureau*. Modernism and urbanism have likewise contributed with migration to the cities and the building of transnational highways, which facilitate the transport of goods and germs. The South African road freight industry, for example, estimates that three truckers a day die from AIDS. War, civil strife, and refugee plight also play their roles: In perhaps the most war-torn country in Africa, the Democratic Republic of Congo, the Great African War has been playing host to several armies highly infected with HIV, including the Zimbabwean army at 80 percent, the Angolan and Congolese armies at 40–60 percent, and the Tanzanian forces at 15–30 percent.

THE IMPACT OF AIDS

The impact of AIDS upon sub-Saharan Africa is also extremely complex and varied. One of the most tragic effects of the AIDS crisis in Africa is the growing number of orphans (see Mary Banda's story below). By 2010, the number of children who have lost one or both parents is estimated to reach 40 million throughout sub-Saharan Africa, which will represent 15 percent of all children on the continent. In those countries that have seen some success in containing AIDS, the disease seems to have engendered a change in behaviors, such as the greater acceptance of condoms and other forms of birth control, endorsement of certain religious and traditional cultures that emphasize strict monogamy and polygamy, and delaying of sexual initiation until marriage. In economic and political terms, AIDS has exacerbated household and nationwide poverty and destabilized administrative bureaucracies through its depletion of the ranks in education, government, and the military. A very crude estimate is that the AIDS crisis costs the sub-Saharan African economy $63.9 billion a year – measured in terms of lost income or purchasing power and health care outlays – which represents 20 percent of Africa's gross national product (GNP). The disease is estimated to be slicing 0.56 to 1.47 percent off the annual growth rate of the African economy, thereby dampening any potential economic expansion.

AIDS COMPARED WITH PAST PANDEMICS

AIDS readily lends itself to comparisons to past pandemics, such as the Black Death. In sub-Saharan Africa, AIDS has produced some remarkably familiar responses. In the Rakai district of Uganda, the sheer number of deaths due to AIDS has forced the villagers to cut short their traditional period of mourning from three or four days to one simply in order to have enough time to attend to agricultural work. There has been no shortage of scapegoats for AIDS, which in sub-Saharan Africa include prostitutes, AIDS widows, and migrant workers from foreign countries. Indeed, on a worldwide stage, Africans as a whole have felt victimized and held unfairly to account for their epidemic. In some areas of Africa, the mysteries and unanswered questions surrounding AIDS, such as why some exposed to HIV become infected and others do not, has led to a resort to explanations of witchcraft and to traditional methods of healing. In South Africa, the AIDS crisis set up a conflict between Western medicine and native agency when President Thabo Mbeki questioned whether HIV was the cause of AIDS and the efficacy of antiretroviral therapies, such as AZT (see his *Letter to World Leaders* below). Instead, Mbeki has declared his preference for an "African solution" to an "African problem" and advanced poverty as the leading cause of AIDS in Africa.

THE EXTRAORDINARY ASPECTS OF AIDS
IN SUB-SAHARAN AFRICA

On the other hand, there are also circumstances undoubtedly unique to the AIDS experience in the sub-Saharan continent. Perhaps due to a combination of historical origins, biological virulence, high risk factors, and absence of medical technologies, AIDS has claimed sub-Saharan Africa for its own, to the point that AIDS may seem to many to be an "African disease." Unlike many other diseases, AIDS in sub-Saharan Africa targets adults in the prime of their lives and has proved particularly devastating for those aged between 15 and 49. It is therefore rapidly sweeping away a whole generation, leaving behind the very young and the very old, both of whom are ill equipped to care for the other. Although AIDS in sub-Saharan Africa certainly feeds on poverty, it also favors the well-to-do, since, ironically, they have the wherewithal to support multiple sex partners. These are some of the very people expected to lead Africa's political and economic development through the next stage of its post-colonial progress. Finally, because of the longevity of those who suffer from AIDS, and because the disease mixes sex and death in a curiously potent partnership, AIDS is playing a role in the continent's history that continues to defy our expectations. Far from being a marginal concern as in wealthier countries of the world, AIDS in sub-Saharan Africa has entered the public consciousness and insinuated itself into its many cultures, where it will remain for some time to come.

SOURCES

AIDS in Uganda: A "Multisectoral" Approach

Uganda was one of the first African countries to report cases of AIDS, in the Rakai district in the southern part of the country in 1981 or 1982. There were several historical and socioeconomic reasons why this was so. As defined by one research team, the contributing factors included the *magendo* economy of the region, which consisted mainly of coffee smuggling; the unequal status of women in society; warfare; and civil unrest. These factors increased migration into and through the region, encouraged women to exchange sex for economic benefits, especially access to land, encouraged sexual promiscuity, and introduced foreign nationals, such as members of the Tanzanian army, with high HIV seroprevalence rates. The bloody, terror-ridden eras of Idi Amin (1971–1979) and Milton Obote (1966–1971 and 1979–1986) were all-around disasters for Uganda and undoubtedly laid the groundwork for the spread of AIDS throughout the country. But origins of the AIDS crisis can be traced even further back to the colonial period under British rule, when a feudal land tenure system was installed in Buganda, a once independent kingdom that later encompassed the Rakai District where AIDS began.

In 1986, Milton Obote was expelled from office and Yoweri Museveni, leader of the National Resistance Movement (NRM), took his place as president of Uganda. This marked a change in policy toward AIDS, in which the political environment became much more welcoming to discussion of and research on the disease. Museveni also took a proactive approach to strategies that might change risk behaviors that were helping to spread AIDS throughout the population, such as launching "love carefully" and "zero grazing" media campaigns. Even as Ugandan scientists deplored Eurocentric views of Africans as highly sexed people who were responsible for the origins of AIDS and who were now to serve as "guinea pigs" for vaccine trials, they still seemed to accept sexual promiscuity as the leading cause of AIDS in Africa, which was distinguished by heterosexual transmission. Yet it should also be pointed out that Museveni has not been entirely consistent in his views on AIDS in Uganda. For example, in December 1990, he blamed his country's AIDS crisis on the "traditions and customary habits, like polygamous marital relations which encouraged the spread of the killer disease," and he claimed that this would necessitate changing "some of our laws which encourage immorality and promiscuity."[2] Nevertheless, just six months later, in his speech in June 1991 before the 7th International Conference on AIDS in Florence, which was to be repeated later that year in November in Kampala, Museveni looked to "a return to our time-tested cultural practices that emphasized fidelity and condemned premarital and extramarital sex" as the "best response to the threat of AIDS and other STDs" (see source selection below). Before 1991, Museveni and other political leaders also indulged in a disturbing tendency to blame prostitutes as scapegoats for the disease. In November 1990, the president declared that the "main route of AIDS is through prostitution," while in December of that year a decree was enacted in one district of Uganda that "any person who practices prostitution commits an offence and on conviction must be sentenced to six months imprisonment, after which she must be deported to her local area of origin."[3] There also has been considerable resistance to advocating condom use, not only by the Museveni government but also by various religious groups, including Catholic, Protestant, Muslim and increasingly more fundamentalist denominations. Religious leaders in Uganda are also more willing to resort to explanations of AIDS as God's punishment for perceived violations of time-honored laws and taboos. Nonetheless, promotion of contraceptives was eventually embraced but only as part of a wider "ABC program" of Abstinence, Being faithful, and Condom use, which has been credited with a dramatic rise to 85 percent condom use in the cities and 50 percent in the countryside.

Overall, Museveni's AIDS policies can claim some dramatic and impressive successes. As of 2003, the prevalence rate of HIV in adults in Uganda stood at 4.1 percent, down from a high of 24.1 percent in the cities and 12.3 percent in the countryside in 1987. Moreover, a detailed survey of HIV infection rates from six sites distributed throughout Uganda found a decline from an average of 23.2 percent in 1991 to 13.6 percent in 1996. Some assert that this decline is simply due to the delayed effect of high mortality from AIDS in Uganda, and it is true that throughout the 1990s, AIDS mortality exceeded HIV incidence in much of the country. Yet the same study also shows that awareness of AIDS and fear of death

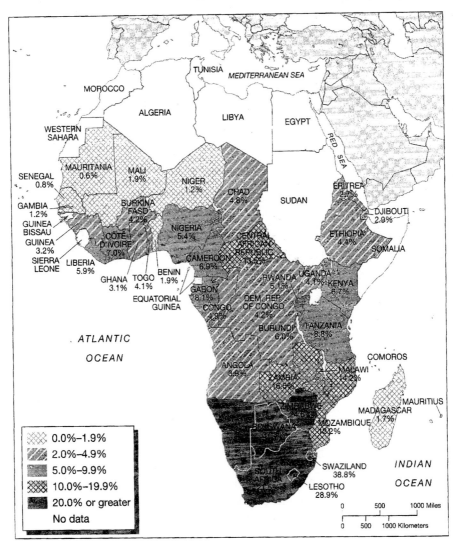

MAP 4.1 HIV prevalence rates in African adults (15–49 years of age) as of the end of 2003.

among communities in Uganda increased, largely as a result of this high mortality. In just 2–3 years, from 1992–1993 to 1995, aware- ness of AIDS as the most common illness in Uganda rose from 44.7 percent of the population to 47.2 percent, while those who knew of at least 11 deaths from AIDS rose from 36.9 percent to 52.1 percent, and of AIDS-related sickness from 21.3 percent to

55 percent. By 1995, more than 86 percent of respondents were worried about the AIDS situation in their communities and affirmed that these feelings differed from those of five years ago. Other indications of behavioral changes as a result of AIDS included that by 1995, more than 44 percent of respondents reported a change in sexual behavior, 56.7 percent of widowers and 77.6 percent of widows had refused to remarry and 71.7 percent expressed a willingness to have an HIV test, down only slightly from 1992–1993, of whom the majority named as the reason for the test to find out whether they were infected by HIV. Other studies indicate that a declining number of children in Uganda have been orphaned by AIDS, down from 37.3 percent in 1992 to 27.4 percent in 1995, but that grandparents rather than surviving mothers were taking on a greater burden of the care of AIDS orphans, and that during the same period, AIDS mortality had been on the rise in northern Uganda, rising from 9 percent in 1982 to 18.5 percent in 1997. This indicates that regional variations with regard to HIV/AIDS incidence do occur in Uganda even as overall rates decline, and reflects probably the delayed arrival of AIDS in the north and the effect of civil unrest there caused by the Lord's Resistance Army (LRA).

Uganda's success in gradually reducing HIV prevalence has now been replicated in several East African countries, most notably in Kenya; but even in Uganda the epidemic remains quite serious. Meanwhile, in West and Central Africa, HIV prevalence levels are in general holding steady at 5 percent or lower, except for Cameroon and Côte d' Ivoire, both at 10 percent prevalence. One of the countries in this region, Senegal, is often cited as the other great "success story" – aside from Uganda – of the struggle against AIDS in sub-Saharan Africa. Here HIV prevalence rates have held steady at 2 percent or less throughout the 1980s and 1990s, and its prevalence is currently under 1 percent; these low rates are largely attributed to a multi-faceted program that includes promotion of condom use and AIDS awareness and prevention in concert with religious groups (Senegal is 93 percent Islamic), compulsory health checks of prostitutes for STDs, screening of blood units for transfusion, and sex education in primary and secondary schools. Senegal also builds on its traditional strengths, such as the emphasis on fidelity even within polygamous marriages, and the high rate of male circumcision in its Muslim communities, which is thought to reduce the risk of contracting STDs and HIV. The results can be seen in a rise to 67 percent condom use among men having casual sex by 1997, a nearly universal use of condoms among commercial sex workers (CSWs), and a nearly 100 percent awareness of AIDS among secondary school students and CSWs. In Zimbabwe in southern Africa, recent surveillance data collected from pregnant women attending antenatal clinics suggest that HIV prevalence and incidence there may have declined over the past five years. This is due to increased condom use in casual sex encounters and reduced rates of sex partner change. Unfortunately, the news from Zimbabwe is a rare bright spot in a generally escalating crisis of HIV/AIDS in southern Africa.

■ Yoweri Museveni, *AIDS is a Socioeconomic Disease*

The following address, *AIDS is a Socioeconomic Disease,* was delivered by Yoweri Museveni, President of Uganda, to the first AIDS Congress in East and Central Africa, held at Kampala, Uganda, on November 20, 1991. This seems to be the same speech that he had given to the 7th International Conference on AIDS at Florence on June 16, 1991. In the first part of his speech, he provides some stark and startling statistics: by 1991, it was estimated that six million people were infected by HIV in sub-Saharan Africa, out of a global population of eight to ten million infected. Museveni then goes on to discuss the historical origins of the disease, its social and economic impact upon Uganda, and how his government has decided to combat AIDS.

As you read this source, keep in mind the following questions. To which socio-cultural factors does Museveni assign blame for AIDS' incursion into Ugandan society – those of Africa or of the West? To what other factor does he assign blame for the sudden appearance of AIDS in sub-Saharan Africa? Why, in his view, does AIDS present such a grave threat to Uganda? Does he regard AIDS as simply a medical problem, or are there larger forces at work? Does he see AIDS as a unique African problem requiring an African solution, or is he open to Western approaches to fighting the disease?

Source: Yoweri K. Museveni, *What is Africa's Problem?,* ed. Elizabeth Kanyogonya (Minneapolis: University of Minnesota Press, 2000), 247–256.

Fertile Ground for the Virus.   While AIDS is the preeminent public health threat of our time, socioeconomic factors crucial in the transmission of the disease and of other sexually transmitted diseases have deep historical roots. In Africa, STDs such as gonorrhea and syphilis were big health hazards before the advent of modern medicine. In order to discourage their spread in society, Africans had evolved cultural taboos against premarital sex and sex out of wedlock. With the advent of sulfas and penicillin, "the magic bullet" of the early 1940s, the fear of STDs subsided, ushering in the era of permissive sexuality. The fear of these diseases changed to indifference: in fact in the 1960s, people here were saying that gonorrhea was like "flu," and self-control was thus thrown by the wayside.

These attitudes were later encouraged by the era of the "sexual revolution" of the 1960s, copied from events in Western Europe, which in turn had been set in motion by the universal availability of the contraceptive pill. All these events culminated in the complete neglect of our traditional herbal and other medicines. In the backward countries, though, because of prevailing socioeconomic circumstances, the promise of the wonder drugs was not to be fulfilled. Although drugs like penicillin were available, STDs were not successfully controlled. . . .

When we are talking about social problems like AIDS, we must bear in mind that its roots lie in the economy. It thus becomes easy to understand that in such a depressed economic environment, expenditure on public health was severely constrained. In Uganda, we have the following distorted ratios:

1 doctor for every 23,000 people, compared to 1 doctor for every 1,000 people in industrialized countries;

1 hospital for every 200,000 people;

1 health unit for every 150,000 people;

1 nurse for every 2,332 people; and

1 health bed facility for every 800 people.

It is, therefore, not surprising that by the early 1970s, STDs had reached epidemic proportions. Studies done showed an incidence of up to 14 percent among mothers attending antenatal clinics in some of our towns. When modern medical facilities are inadequate, STDs are usually not diagnosed at all, or if they are, they are not properly treated. . . .

In view of the socioeconomic factors enumerated above, it is not surprising that when HIV arrived in East and Central Africa in the early 1980s, it landed on fertile ground. It is like the parable of the seeds in the Bible: one dropped on the rock; one fell by the wayside; but like the seed that fell on fertile ground, when HIV came to this region, it fell on fertile ground indeed! The AIDS epidemic has demonstrated the historical continuity of the social, political, and medical reaction of epidemics among socially deprived populations. A historical appreciation of the resilience of the social conditions that promote disease like AIDS may help society in responding rationally to protect the public's health.

A Thin Piece of Rubber. Epidemiological studies have traditionally focused on the biological dynamics of disease, such as the incubation period, infectiousness of the disease organism, and its ability to cause death. AIDS has, more than any other disease, brought about the recognition that the spread of the disease may be driven more by sociological and economic dynamics. AIDS cannot be understood in biological terms alone. Sex is not a simple manifestation of a biological drive; it is socially dictated. The sexual opportunities available to an individual and the type of partners deemed appropriate will vary from one social group to another. It is in view of this background that I have been emphasizing a return to our time-tested cultural practices that emphasized fidelity and condemned premarital and extramarital sex. I believe that the best response to the threat of AIDS and other STDs is to reaffirm publicly and forthrightly the respect and responsibility every person owes to his or her neighbor. Just as we were offered the "magic bullet" in the early 1940s, we are now being offered the condom for "safe sex." We are being told that only a thin piece of rubber stands between us and the death of our continent. I feel that condoms have a role to play as a means of protection, especially in couples who are HIV-positive, but they cannot become the main means of stemming the tide of AIDS.

I am not against the use of the condom, but if it were available, affordable, and if our people knew how to use it, then it would be up to them to protect themselves. We have not banned condoms, but we caution: these people to whom you are advocating the use of condoms may not be able to use them properly. . . . Condoms are not the way out in a population that is 90 percent peasant and largely illiterate. Instead of wasting money on condoms on a mass scale, you should buy more AIDS testing equipment to reach the villages so that young people who are getting married should first test their blood. . . .

An Economic and Social Catastrophe. AIDS was first recognized in Uganda in 1981, but because of the negative feelings and sensationalism that surrounded the subject, the government of the day decided to bury its head in the sand like the proverbial ostrich. A lot of time was, therefore, lost between 1981 and 1986, when we got into government. Our government has had no qualms about being frank to our people on issues of a national catastrophe such as the AIDS epidemic. When we came to power in 1986, the problem had already spread to most parts of the country. We opened the gates to national and international efforts aimed at controlling the epidemic. Unfortunately, despite my government's efforts and the high level of awareness among the population, the AIDS epidemic is becoming more and more serious in Uganda. However, this awareness has, over the last few years, started paying off. I am informed that there has been a marked decline in the incidence of other STDs. AIDS has, however, hit hardest those who are not only in their most sexually active years, but also in their most economically productive years. A decline in the labor force is already being experienced at both the national and household levels. A number of professionals working in government and other institutions have died. In our countries, where education and technical expertise are at a premium, this will cancel out our economic and social gains.

For many rural households, current levels of agricultural production may be threatened, especially as agricultural activities are labor-intensive. This will affect production by smallholders, which accounts for over 90 percent of our country's export earnings. The reduction will cause more economic strain, especially when coffee prices are not favorable. With regard to social services, AIDS is already affecting our overstretched medical services. Apart from looking after AIDS patients, secondary infections such as tuberculosis (TB) have increased because of AIDS. . . .

An Integrated Sectoral Approach.   In Uganda, we have realized that the AIDS problem goes beyond the mere health of people. We have, therefore, adopted a multisectoral strategy for the control of the epidemic. Where control measures were previously centered in the health sector, we are now establishing fully fledged control programs in other key sectors of communication, rehabilitation, education, community services, defense, and economic planning. An independent body, the Uganda AIDS Commission, has been established to guide, direct, coordinate, and monitor the strategy. The commission will monitor the control measures of the various sectors by listening to the voices of the people through its field officers and grassroots leaders. This strategy will be able to harness our efforts in combating AIDS. . . .

Develop Herbal Medicines.   Uganda's and Africa's forests and savannahs still conserve the largest variety of plant and animal life. These are a potential source of natural chemotherapeutics for AIDS and other diseases. When we became aware of the possibility of using natural herbs in the treatment of HIV, some of the modern doctors laughed at us. My line was that since modern medicine has no answer to this problem, let us encourage our people to carry out their own research either by scientific methods or by empirical observation. Our people here have observed the use of herbs for a very long time, and by discouraging them, I am sure we are doing a disservice to humanity. You might find that the salvation for mankind may come from these people you despise. . . .

Although I am talking about carrying out research locally so that we can help our people, our emphasis has been in health education and change of sexual behavior, having realized that HIV infection is mostly dependent on voluntary behavior, unlike most other transmittable diseases. Even so, we shall ultimately depend on the concerted efforts of you scientists, in your various disciplines, to lead us out of this dark abyss.

AIDS in South Africa: The Tragedy of Denial

If Uganda is a success story in how to combat AIDS even in a poor country with few resources, then the Republic of South Africa, blessed with the second highest per capita income in sub-Saharan Africa, at over $3,000 per year, and a country with one of the highest government expenditures on health, at 11.6 percent of its budget, is a tragic story of missed opportunities and inexplicable inertia. Moreover, South Africa has one of the most liberal democratic constitutions of any country in Africa, if not the world, ever since it cast off its apartheid regime in 1994. But as of 2003, South Africa had an HIV prevalence rate of 21.5 percent, with a total number of infected individuals at over 5 million, giving it the dubious distinction of having the largest population of people living with HIV of any country in the world. Moreover, its mortality rate from AIDS has been rapidly approaching half a million deaths a year. What went wrong?

Like anywhere with a high incidence of the disease, South Africa's AIDS crisis is the product of many factors. For example, despite a progressive constitution that enshrines protections for women, South Africa has one of the highest recorded rates of rape in the world, 12.5 per 10,000 people as of 2001, compared to 3.2 per 10,000 in the United States. Obviously, this is a product of a somewhat intangible but quite real cultural and socioeconomic gender inequality that cannot simply be legislated out of existence. Aside from an inability to negotiate safe sex practices or partner fidelity, women in South Africa also face unique cultural pressures to engage in vaginal "dry sex," particularly among adolescents, which puts them at extremely high risk for HIV transmission. Despite having a relatively high per capita income, South Africa possesses one of the most unequal distributions of that income on the continent, which ensures that much of the black African population is mired in poverty. Colonialism has left South Africa with a legacy of migrant labor, particularly among workers in the gold and diamond mines, which goes hand-in-hand with prostitution and resort to multiple sex partners. South Africa also has a legacy of intervention in wars in neighboring countries, such as Angola, which may have resulted in high HIV infection rates among its newly reconstituted South African National Defense Force (SANDF). But it is the political context and controversy surrounding the government's policy toward AIDS that has attracted the most attention and comment concerning South Africa's current crisis with the disease.

From 1982, when the first AIDS cases in South Africa were reported, until 1994, the ruling National Party's policy toward AIDS was severely hampered by the politics of apartheid and, beginning in 1989, rapid but painful transition to a true democratic government. Despite attempts at AIDS education, monitoring, training, counseling, research, and advertising, the apartheid state was utterly unable to gain the trust and cooperation of its black majority, and the African National Congress (ANC) and other anti-apartheid groups pursued a policy of non-collaboration as well as their own, alternative AIDS campaigns. The conservative movement in South Africa did not help itself by using the threat of AIDS as an excuse to call for renewed segregation, to scapegoat homosexuals, and, apparently, to even celebrate the disease as a wedge against black majority rule. It is hard to see how the government could succeed when it was both criticized for promoting condom use and safe sex – as part of a "genocidal" program to halt reproduction among blacks – and for not doing enough to protect people against AIDS – again as part of an alleged conspiracy to control black population growth. Indeed, conspiracy theories concerning the apartheid government and AIDS did abound: on the one hand that the virus was intentionally manufactured and spread among the black population, and on the other that the disease was entirely fabricated as a scare tactic, according to which AIDS should really stand for "Afrikaner Invention to Deprive us of Sex". With its hands tied, largely through the fault of its own oppressive policies toward its black subjects, the apartheid regime limped along to an unlamented demise, and all eyes looked to the ANC government for a new start on AIDS policy.

Any hopes for a unified and progressive policy toward AIDS under the leadership of South Africa's legendary new president, Nelson Mandela, quickly evaporated into disillusionment. Shortly after ANC came to power in April 1994, a comprehensive and widely praised National AIDS Plan was adopted, yet it was never given the priority of a program operating directly out of the office of the president, in contrast to Uganda's "multisectoral" approach that was spearheaded by Yoweri Museveni. Instead, the plan was allowed to languish in the Department of Health, which many felt did not do justice to the disease's wide-ranging impact, while Mandela failed to provide the leadership so desperately needed in the crisis. Two scandals also marred the government's efforts against AIDS: one was the commissioning of a musical with an anti-AIDS message, *Sarafina II*, which gobbled up 14.2 million Rand (a bit more than 2 million U.S. dollars) of an already thinly-stretched AIDS budget, and the other was the endorsement of a toxic chemical, an industrial solvent given the brand name Virodene, as a treatment for AIDS. At the same time, the health ministry under Dr. Nkosazana Dlamini-Zuma refused to make a proven antiretroviral drug, AZT, available to provincial health clinics, despite the fact that AZT, aside from prolonging the life span of AIDS patients, had a 50 percent success rate in preventing transmission of HIV from mother to child, and despite that the drug's American manufacturer, Glaxo Wellcome, was willing to drastically cut its price for the South African market. Meanwhile, AIDS was becoming a major health threat: Although the disease was late in coming to South Africa, it was rapidly spreading among the population, nearly doubling or trebling every two years – from 0.7 percent in 1990, to 2.2 percent in 1992, 7.6 percent in 1994, and 14.2 percent in 1996.

By far the most bizarre and controversial twist in South Africa's AIDS saga was yet to come. In 1999, the election of a new ANC president, Thabo Mbeki, and appointment of a new minister of Health, Dr. Manto Tshabalala-Msimang, seemed to promise a fresh start on

AIDS policy, but the result was to be for the worse. Claiming to have done research on his own on the Internet, President Mbeki – who had earlier championed Virodene – came out against AZT as a potentially toxic drug and even called into question "the science of AIDS," by which he meant that he was siding with AIDS "dissidents" who disputed the existence of HIV, AIDS, and, indeed, of a disease crisis occurring anywhere in Africa. Since AIDS behaves differently in Africa than in other parts of the world, Mbeki declared his preference for "an African solution to an African problem," in that he viewed AIDS deaths as primarily caused by poverty rather than a specific viral agent, and therefore the battle had to be fought on social rather than biological grounds. Before Mbeki withdrew his voice, but not his influence, from the AIDS debate in 2002, he made his views known in three communications: an address in March 2000 to a Presidential Advisory Panel on AIDS – notorious for its inclusion of dissident scientists on equal footing to the "orthodox" who accepted HIV as the cause of AIDS; an extraordinary letter to world leaders in April of that year (see source selection below); and an address in July to the 13th International AIDS Conference in Durban. Dissident scientific views on AIDS are based on claims that HIV fails to fulfill protocols for its identification as a disease organism, doubts that are perhaps exacerbated by the failure of the medical community to so far find a vaccine or cure, while the nutritionist Roberto Giraldo dismisses sexual transmission of HIV as a myth and claims that the disease can be prevented or even treated by healthy diet alone. Historians like Charles Geshekter and Richard and Rosalind Chirimutta are also prepared to challenge mainstream scientific views on AIDS, such as that it originated in Africa, on the grounds that a racist "association of black people with dirt, disease, ignorance and an animal-like sexual promiscuity" is the basis for such views, whereas poverty as the direct cause of AIDS provides convincing confirmation of the historical inequity visited upon black Africans. Mbeki himself was not above hiding behind old, anti-apartheid rhetoric in defense of his "denialist" position, which he cast as an attempt to provide open debate and dissent. A sarcastic e-mail that Mbeki circulated among the National Executive Council of the ANC in March 2002 demonstrated how racially righteous hyperbole could be drafted into the service of a stonewalling AIDS policy:

Yes, we are sex crazy! Yes we are diseased! Yes, we spread the deadly HI virus through our uncontrolled heterosexual sex! In this regard, yes, we are different from the US and Western Europe! Yes, we, the men, abuse women and the girl-child with gay abandon! Yes, among us rape is endemic because of our culture! Yes, we do believe that sleeping with young virgins will cure us of AIDS! Yes, as a result of all this, we are threatened with destruction by the HIV/AIDS pandemic! Yes, what we need, and cannot afford because we are poor, are condoms and anti-retroviral drugs! Help![4]

Mbeki has been opposed in his denialist AIDS position by a galaxy of scientists, politicians, and activists. On July 6, 2000, the "Durban Declaration" signed by 5,000 scientists within and outside South Africa tried to set the scientific record straight on HIV and AIDS, but was dismissed by Tshabalala-Msimang as an "elitist document". At the International AIDS Conference that began four days later in Durban, Edwin Cameron, an HIV-positive High Court judge, lambasted the Mbeki government for sowing "confusion among those at risk of HIV and consternation amongst AIDS workers" through his "flirtation" with dissident views, which he characterized as bordering on "criminality." In July 2000 Tony Leon, leader of the opposition Democratic Party, conducted a debate by public correspondence with Mbeki in which he refuted accusations that denialist opponents were in the pocket of pharmaceutical companies and accused Mbeki in turn of attempting to coopt dissent by resorting to charges of racism and of imposing his own "dogma" in place of the scientific consensus he was seeking to destroy. By February 2002, even members of Mbeki's government began to defy him, as his minister of Home Affairs, Mangosuthu Buthelezi, leader of the Inkatha Freedom Party, an important ANC ally, came out in support of the decision by his home province, KwaZulu-Natal, to administer the antiretroviral drug Nevirapine to infected pregnant women despite a government ban. Perhaps the most concerted opposition has come from an AIDS activist group, the Treatment Action Campaign (TAC), led by Zackie Achmat. In August 2001, TAC took the Mbeki government to court for failing to implement a mother-to-child-transmission (MTCT) prevention program using antiretroviral therapies, on the grounds that it violated the South African Bill of Rights that guaranteed every child "the right to basic healthcare services." In December, judgment was handed down by the Pretoria High Court against the government, later upheld in July 2002 by the national Constitutional Court. Although the government seemed to back down on its resistance to antiretrovirals in April 2002, as of 2003, it still had not implemented the MTCT program and Achmat had organized a civil disobedience campaign and his own personal antiretroviral "drug strike" to force Mbeki to change his mind. Shortly before the 2004 national elections, the Mbeki cabinet did announce a MTCT treatment program, but its implementation remains unclear and has not been given a high priority in the budget. Most striking, perhaps, is how a country that managed to miraculously heal itself of a bitterly entrenched racial divide, then almost immediately embarked upon another rift – completely unnecessary – over AIDS policy. For those who can afford and access treatment, and for those who cannot, AIDS is the new apartheid of a politically free South Africa.

■ Thabo Mbeki, Letter to World Leaders, April 3, 2000

On April 3, 2000, Thabo Mbeki, president of South Africa, hand-addressed the following letter to U.S. President Bill Clinton, British Prime Minister Tony Blair, and U.N. Secretary-General Kofi Annan. The letter seeks to defend the controversial policy toward AIDS of the Mbeki government, which has been accused of stonewalling the use of antiretroviral (ARV) treatments, such as the drug AZT, despite the fact that ARVs have been proven to be effective in slowing transmission of the disease from mother to child during pregnancy and in prolonging the life span of AIDS patients. Although Mbeki in his letter does not explicitly deny that HIV causes AIDS, he does vigorously defend "dissident" scientists who have taken that position, and he pointedly included such "dissidents" in his Presidential Advisory Panel on AIDS, to whom he addressed another public statement on AIDS policy on the occasion of its first meeting at Pretoria on May 6. Perhaps in order to justify his government's isolated position, Mbeki is at pains in his letter to define the incidence of AIDS in Africa as a uniquely African problem, and thus one that requires an African – not Western – solution. In his address to the 13th annual International AIDS Conference, held at Durban, South Africa, on July 9, Mbeki also pursued another theme from his letter, in which he identified the leading culprit in his country's health crisis as poverty – not AIDS – a cause that obviously entails a social or cultural response, rather than a medical or scientific one.

As you read this document, compare Mbeki's views and policies with those of Yoweri Museveni (see above). What positions do they share and where do they differ? Is Mbeki justified in claiming to be persecuted for his unusual stance on AIDS? Why or why not? How do you think the government's stance will affect South African citizens infected or yet to be infected by HIV?

I am honoured to convey to you the compliments of our government as well as my own, and to inform you about some work we are doing to respond to the HIV-AIDS epidemic.

As you are aware, international organizations such as UNAIDS have been reporting that sub-Saharan Africa accounts for two-thirds of the world incidence of HIV-AIDS. These reports indicate that our own country is among the worst affected. Responding to these reports, in 1998, our government decided radically to step up its own efforts to combat AIDS, this fight having, up to this point, been left largely to our Ministry and Department of Health. Among other things, we set up a Ministerial Task Force against HIV-AIDS chaired by the Deputy President of the Republic, which position I was privileged to occupy at the time. Our current Deputy President, the Hon. Jacob Zuma, now leads this Task Force.

We also established Partnerships against AIDS, with many major sectors of our society including the youth, women, business, labour unions and the religious communities. We have now also established a National AIDS Council, again chaired by the Deputy President and bringing together the government and civil society. An important part of the campaign that we are conducting seeks to encourage safe sex and the use of condoms. At the same time, as an essential part of our campaign against HIV-AIDS, we are working to ensure that we focus properly and urgently on the elimination of poverty among the millions of our people. Similarly, we are doing everything we can, within our very limited possibilities, to provide the necessary medicaments and care to deal with what are described as "opportunistic diseases" that attach to acquired immune deficiency.

Source: www.virusmyth.com.

As a government and a people, we are trying to organize ourselves to ensure that we take care of the children affected and orphaned to AIDS. We work also to ensure that no section of our society, whether public or private, discriminates against people suffering from HIV-AIDS. In our current budget, we have included a dedicated fund to finance our activities against HIV-AIDS. This is in addition to funds that the central government departments as well as the provincial and local administrations will spend on this campaign. We have also contributed to our Medical Research Council such funds as we can, for the development of an AIDS vaccine.

Demands are being made within the country of the public health system to provide anti-retroviral drugs for various indications, including mother-to-child transmission. We are discussing this matter, among others, with our statutory licensing authority for medicines and drugs, the Medicines Control Council (MCC). Toward the end of last year, speaking in our national parliament, I said that I had asked our Minister of Health to look into various controversies taking place among scientists on HIV-AIDS and the toxicity of a particular anti-retroviral drug [AZT]. In response to this, among other things, the Minister is working to put together an international panel of scientists to discuss all these issues in as transparent a setting as possible.

As you know, AIDS in the United States and other developed Western countries has remained largely confined to a section of the male homosexual population. .... Again as you are aware, whereas in the West HIV-AIDS is said to be largely homosexually transmitted, it is reported that in Africa, including our country, it is transmitted heterosexually.

Accordingly, as Africans, we have to deal with this uniquely African catastrophe that:

- contrary to the West, HIV-AIDS in Africa is heterosexually transmitted;
- contrary to the West, where relatively few people have died from AIDS, itself a matter of serious concern, millions are said to have died in Africa; and,
- contrary to the West, where AIDS deaths are declining, even greater numbers of Africans are destined to die.

It is obvious that whatever lessons we have to and may draw from the West about the grave issue of HIV-AIDS, a simple superimposition of Western experience on African reality would be absurd and illogical.

Such proceeding would constitute a criminal betrayal of our responsibility to our own people. It was for this reason that I spoke as I did in our parliament, in the manner in which I have indicated.

I am convinced that our urgent task is to respond to the specific threat that faces us as Africans. We will not eschew this obligation in favour of the comfort of the recitation of a catechism that may very well be a correct response to the specific manifestation of AIDS in the West. We will not, ourselves, condemn our own people to death by giving up the search for specific and targeted responses to the specifically African incidence of HIV-AIDS. I make these comments because our search for these specific and targeted responses is being stridently condemned by some in our country and the rest of the world as constituting a criminal abandonment of the fight against HIV-AIDS.

Some elements of this orchestrated campaign of condemnation worry me very deeply. It is suggested, for instance, that there are some scientists who are "dangerous and discredited" with whom nobody, including ourselves, should communicate or interact. In an earlier period in human history, these would be heretics that would be burnt at the stake!

Not long ago, in our own country, people were killed, tortured, imprisoned and prohibited from being quoted in private and in public because the established authority believed that their views were dangerous and discredited. We are now being asked to do precisely the same thing that the racist apartheid tyranny we opposed did, because, it is said, there exists a scientific view that is supported by the majority, against which dissent is prohibited.

The scientists we are supposed to put into scientific quarantine include Nobel Prize Winners, Members of Academies of Science and Emeritus Professors of various disciplines of medicine! Scientists, in the name of science, are demanding that we should cooperate with them to freeze scientific discourse on HIV-AIDS at the specific point this discourse had reached in the West in 1984.

People who otherwise would fight very hard to defend the critically important rights of freedom of thought and speech occupy, with regard to the HIV-AIDS issue, the frontline in the campaign of intellectual intimidation and terrorism which argues that the only freedom we have is to agree with what they decree to be established scientific truths. Some agitate for these extraordinary propositions with a religious fervour borne by a degree of fanaticism, which is truly frightening.

The day may not be far off when we will, once again, see books burnt and their authors immolated by fire by those who believe that they have a duty to conduct a holy crusade against the infidels. It is most strange that all of us seem ready to serve the cause of the fanatics by deciding to stand and wait.

It may be that these comments are extravagant. If they are, it is because in the very recent past, we had to fix our own eyes on the very face of tyranny.

I am greatly encouraged that all of us, as Africans, can count on your unwavering support in the common fight to save our continent and its peoples from death from AIDS.

Voices of AIDS: The Disease's Impact upon Women and Children

The AIDS crisis in sub-Saharan Africa, while hard on all those touched – directly or indirectly – by its overmighty reach, is especially so on women and children. Scapegoats of the disease tend to be female, such as prostitutes and other commercial sex workers, female migrants and traders, and widows, who are blamed for the deaths of their partners and shunned by their relatives and communities until they are forced to migrate, thus, ironically, widening the spread of the epidemic. Economic inequities also fall disproportionately hard on sub-Saharan African women, whether it be disinheritance, lower wages and employment prospects, or lack of autonomy over family finances. These circumstances often force women – even those not regarded as prostitutes or commercial sex workers – into negotiating their sexual favors for economic rewards, usually in the form of money or land, in a kind of barter or transactional relationship. Women surveyed in KwaZulu-Natal in South Africa, for example, cited the need for multiple sexual partners just to survive economically and make ends meet: "One [boyfriend] for rent, one for food, and one for clothes." Female students at Makerere University in Kampala, Uganda, also testified to having three partners, one their "sugar daddy" (for books and other necessities), another their teacher (for good grades), and a third, their generationally-compatible boyfriend.

Social and cultural factors also heavily discourage sub-Saharan African women from negotiating safe sex practices with their partners, such as using condoms. A survey of HIV positive and negative pregnant women in southern Uganda found the vast majority unwilling to use condoms outright, or only if their husbands approved. The most popular reasons cited for saying no to condoms included concerns about health side effects (such as fears condoms might break inside the vagina), concerns about their use as a sign of sexual promiscuity or lack of trust in the husband, and concerns about their effectiveness or inability to use them properly. There is also great pressure upon sub-Saharan African women to prove their fertility and ability to produce children within a marriage. On the man's side, there is often great resistance to using condoms as inhibiting sexual pleasure ("like eating candy with the wrapper on") or great fatalism toward the risks of contracting AIDS ("let it take me because I cannot keep from the young girls"). In addition there is the grim reality of sexual violence and coercion, which especially targets younger women. Nor should we omit to consider cultural pressures upon women unique to certain sub-Saharan African countries. For example, in South Africa, Zambia, and the Democratic Republic of Congo there is the tradition of using "dry sex" to enhance male sexual pleasure – which can irritate the vaginal membranes, leaving the women more susceptible to HIV infection. In South Africa there is also an insistence upon virginity testing, which makes adolescent girls vulnerable to older men who may believe that sex with a virgin can cure AIDS, or that intercourse with younger women carries less risk of HIV infection. (One survey in South Africa found that 7 percent of respondents believed one could be cured of AIDS by having sex with a virgin, 12 percent believed one could get HIV/AIDS from condoms, and 13 percent believed that traditional African medicine had a cure for AIDS.) In Botswana, widows are easy targets as scapegoats for *boswagadi*, a belief that life-threatening conditions such as AIDS are caused by violation of sexual taboos after the death of the husband.

The entrenchment of these social, cultural, and economic norms that put sub-Saharan African women at higher risk for AIDS can be rather daunting and depressing, yet there are scattered signs of changes in behaviors in the wake of and as a response to the disease crisis. In Durban, South Africa, and in the Ovambo- and Kavango-speaking regions of Namibia, women expressed an emphatic desire to see demonstrations of and have access to female condoms from visiting AIDS experts as a way to protect themselves from HIV. In Tanzania and Zambia, various women's clubs, community groups, and non-governmental organizations (NGOs) have been formed to raise AIDS awareness and empower and support women caught up in the crisis. An intervention program in Nigeria found that commercial sex workers, commercial drivers, and students were very receptive to using condoms if these were provided along with instruction on their use and benefits. Clearly, a change in both collective cultures and individual behaviors – among both men and women – will be required if the AIDS epidemic in sub-Saharan Africa is to be brought under control.

The direct impact of AIDS on children in sub-Saharan Africa includes the creation of orphans when one or both parents die of the disease, and the infection of children through mother-to-child-transmission (MTCT) or through adolescent intercourse. (In South Africa, for example, the typical age for sexual initiation is 12 for girls and 14 for boys.) The orphan crisis is perhaps of greatest concern, since it is growing so rapidly and incorporates many children infected with HIV. If orphans are defined as those who have lost both parents or their mother, then the number is expected to grow from 13 million in 2000, to 24 million in 2010, and 40 million in 2020. If paternal orphans are included, the 40 million mark is expected to be reached by 2010. As of 1999, five countries in southern Africa – Mozambique, Malawi, South Africa, Zambia, and Zimbabwe – had between them well over 2.5 million orphans, the majority of whom were orphaned by AIDS. Since the 15–49 age bracket is most at risk for contracting AIDS, this implies a generational shift in Africa's population, where the very old will care for the very young and the number of child-headed households will increase. A 1999 census in South Africa found that 40 percent of its population comprises children under the age of 18, while in Botswana, it is estimated that adults in their 60s and 70s will outnumber those in their 40s and 50s by 2020.

Tradition in sub-Saharan Africa dictates that the extended family care for orphans, and some cultures even sanction child fostering by the biological parents during their lifetimes. However, this custom is being sorely tested, and indeed overwhelmed, by the sheer numbers of orphans created by AIDS. Add to this the fact that extended families may already be spending much of their income to care for adult AIDS patients, and this safety net for orphans seems in danger of collapse under the combined burdens created by the disease. One study conducted in 1997 in northern Uganda found that, after a surviving parent, orphans were most often cared for by grandparents or by an older sibling, also an orphan. Moreover, fewer extended family members were stepping in to provide care, so that, for the first time, orphanages and NGOs might have to take a major role in alleviating the crisis.

In such circumstances, the indirect impacts of AIDS on orphans are also dire. These include poor nutrition and health, high drop-out rates from school (particularly so for girls, for whom there are higher expectations as caregivers), poverty, child migration and labor, and higher exposure to HIV from sexual exploitation or prostitution. Nor can psychological effects, such as depression, anxiety, and ridicule, be dismissed, even if they are harder to measure. Studies in Uganda and Zambia found that children were more prone to isolation, sadness, worry, anger, despair, and low expectations for the future when their parents became sick with AIDS. On top of all this, AIDS orphans also faced stigmatization and discrimination from their peers, which naturally intensified their trauma and stress. If children are the future of a country, then many places in sub-Saharan Africa have cause for great concern – and for urgent action – in the coming decades as more and more of their children are orphaned by AIDS.

■ Two Women's Stories: Mary Banda of Zambia and Dambudzo of Zimbabwe

The following are two women's accounts of their personal struggles with AIDS and its impact on their families. One, Mary Banda, is a widowed grandmother who lives in a small brick house on the northwestern outskirts of Lusaka, Zambia's capital city. There, she cares for eight of her orphaned grandchildren, ranging in age from six to twenty. Mary Banda herself is referred to as one of the "elderly orphaned," so named because by 2000, five of her eight children had died from AIDS, one a year for five years running, leaving her alone to care for her grandchildren. At that time, Mary Banda was estimated to be about 65 years old. The second subject, a young married woman named Dambudzo, discovered she had AIDS in 1987, just after the birth of her third child, who later died of the disease in 1989, when her interview took place. At that time, Dambudzo was living in Harare, the capital of Zimbabwe, and was active in the Mashambanzou AIDS Crisis Center. In each of these countries, the HIV prevalence rate as of 2003 was 16.5 percent for Zambia and 24.6 percent for Zimbabwe; Zambia currently has about half a million women living with HIV, while Zimbabwe has close to a million.

Some questions relevant to their stories include the following: How does each woman explain the cause of the predicament posed by AIDS to themselves and their families? Could this predicament have been avoided? How have their families experienced the social, economic, and psychological effects of the AIDS pandemic? How has each woman chosen to respond to the challenges wrought by AIDS?

Mary Banda.   My son, the oldest of my eight children, Tamanga, died first. He didn't have any children. Then there was Jennifer, and she also died. Her children are Mapala and Chikabvemka. My third child was Olio, mother of Abraham and David. My fourth child was Anna. She died leaving two children but they're staying with other relatives. Malawi, my fifth child, had Ruth, Eva, James and Bernard. . . .

When my children became sick, I took them to traditional healers, as well as to the hospital. It was the witchdoctors who told me they'd been bewitched in the village, but they didn't say by whom. The government has made a ruling that traditional healers shouldn't tell people that so-and-so bewitched their child because it causes fights. *Mbuyas* [grandmothers] like me must try not to be bitter that people have killed our children and now we have to look after orphans. We shouldn't try and seek vengeance on those people. Vengeance is for the Lord.

I used to just look after two grandchildren, because it's traditional in Zambia to keep some grandchildren even when their parents are alive. But when my children started dying, all these other children started moving in. It was OK at first because my other offspring were helping. The real problems began when I no longer had children able to help, and more and more grandchildren needing to move in. . . .

The children's biggest problem is getting enough food. Sometimes I sell groundnuts by the road. Those who are feeling sorry give me some money. But it's not enough. We try to grow some maize, sweet potato and greens so we have two meals a day. The older boys have been very helpful in the garden. They don't mind. When my children were sick I couldn't go to the fields, so they were doing most of the work then. And Ruth helps me with the cooking and washing plates and taking care of little Eva. Only James and Ruth are in school and even they are sometimes chased away because they don't have shoes, fees or uniforms. . . .

Sources: Emma Guest, *Children of AIDS: Africa's Orphan Crisis,* 2nd edition (London and Pietermaritzburg, SA: Pluto Press and University of Natal Press, 2003), 19–22; *Positive Women: Voices of Women Living with AIDS,* eds. Andrea Rudd and Darien Taylor (Toronto: Second Story Press, 1992), 169–171.

I like to go to church and meet my friends. We share problems, and it makes you realize you're not the only one. There are lots of people in the same position as me. I also get help from an organization called Children in Distress Widows' Support Group. Once a month they give me some mealie meal [maize], beans and cooking oil, but it's not enough because the boys are eating all the time. When all the deaths were happening, friends from church would cook for the people coming to the funerals. Neighbors raised some money to get a few planks to make up the coffins, and some women from Children in Distress came and comforted me.

I'm an old woman who's suffering. When I was young, I never thought such cruel things could happen. When I think about it, I pray and cry, but I don't like to cry because it'll upset the children. The church has given me the strength to go on because I know that one day I'll die too and join my children.

Dambudzo.   In 1986, I got married to a caretaker. This caretaker of mine was working at the church. I trusted him very much and thought I had made a good choice to marry a Christian. But to my surprise this husband of mine was quite different from what I thought. This man wasn't satisfied with one woman. He used to go to the Borrowdale Racetrack for betting. When I was six months pregnant, my problems started. I told my husband that it was time for me to go to the prenatal clinic. He said, "This month I don't have enough money. You will go next month." When another month was finished, he said the same thing as before. . . .

That's how my problem started. When we stayed together during my pregnancy, he was attacked by VD [venereal disease] about six times, but he refused to go to the doctor. When I was seven months pregnant the Lord came to help me. God provided the reverend's wife who came to me and asked me if I was attending the prenatal clinic. I replied that we didn't have money. She said, "Tomorrow, I will take you there." . . .

After everything was done, I was told that my blood was negative for syphilis. What a big surprise, since I was sleeping with my husband who had all those sores. If I had said no, he would have said, "Pack your things and go right now, at midnight. If you tell anybody that I am sick then don't come back. Stay away forever." Where would I go while I was seven months pregnant?

Indeed, I was in real trouble for sure. I tried to tell the nurse. I explained how he was sick. The nurse said, "Tell him to come here." I told him but he said, "No. I will not go. I will rather go to the *n'anga* (traditional healer), than the doctor." I went and told the nurse again. Then she said, "Now we can't help you because your blood was negative. If it was positive for syphilis, we could force your husband to get treated." . . .

Suddenly on June 11 I went into labor. I was a mother of two already, but the pain of this third pregnancy was quite different from the others. I delivered the baby at 2:00 a.m., after 12 hours of suffering. By the time I delivered, I was breathing by means of oxygen. The baby was 3,320 grams. A healthy baby everybody said, but nobody knew that the HIV had been passed from father to mother to this otherwise healthy baby.

We came to know this when I was seriously sick after the birth of the baby. I stayed at home for only seven days. On the eighth day, I was admitted to Parirenyatwa Hospital. I had abdominal pain, diarrhea, vomiting, chest pain, swelling and tenderness in every part of my body, and I felt very weak. The abdominal pain was coming in intervals, just as though I was going to deliver another baby. Maybe there was another baby about to come out. I even mentioned it to the doctor and said the pain was just the same as labor pain. This is the most terrible disease I have ever had in my life time.

After so many examinations and blood tests, I was told on July 7, 1987 that I was carrying the HIV in my blood. I was shocked, because I didn't understand it as I do now. I thought that it was the end of my life. I even gave all that belonged to me with [sic] my relatives. And so many people are still saying there is no AIDS. They are fooling themselves for sure.

Voices of Resistance: Two AIDS Activists
■ **Speeches of Rosemary Mulenga of Zambia and Nkosi Johnson of South Africa**

Here follow excerpts from the speeches of two people – both HIV positive – who have been active in the struggle to improve the quality of life of African women and orphaned children living with AIDS. One is a married woman and mother of four children, Rosemary Mulenga, who was diagnosed with AIDS in 1987, along with her husband and five-year-old son. She delivered her speech in 1990 at the 3rd International AIDS Conference, held in Paris, France. The second speech was made by an 11-year-old boy, Nkosi Johnson, at the 13th International AIDS Conference, held in 2000 at Durban, South Africa. Xolani Nkosi Johnson was born in a slum township of Johannesburg, capital of South Africa, and his mother, Nonthlanthla Daphne Nkosi, died of AIDS in 1997. At the age of 12 and weighing just 20 pounds, Nkosi Johnson died of brain complications from his disease on June 1, 2001. It is expected that the number of AIDS orphans in South Africa will peak at 1.85 million in 2015.

What issues are identified by each of these activists as crucial in the fight against AIDS? How are they each critical of their respective government's policies with regard to the disease? How is each of these AIDS victims fighting back? How does their testimony relate to the women's stories in the sources above?

Rosemary Mulenga. I consider myself to be an average middle class Zambian woman. My husband Oliver is a journalist. I used to work as a teacher. We are no different from other Zambian families except that we are HIV positive. I was diagnosed positive in January 1987 after being ill for about four months with hepatitis B. My husband and my now five-year-old son were also found positive. We were shocked and anxiety filled our lives: fear of early death and especially who will look after our four children if we died. You know, those sort of questions became real to us. We have not been courageous enough to tell our children about it yet. We have managed to tell our parents and brothers and sisters and a few friends, although they would not accept it as true. We have received a lot of support from the church and the support group to which I belong.

Since my condition, my life has become more real and fruitful. I and my husband have helped to form an HIV/AIDS support group in the city of Lusaka. About 20 people meet every Saturday to support one another. I am involved in giving educational talks to church women and school children on AIDS and I try to get them involved in the care of the sick and children in distress. I believe that God has given me a message for the church and other organizations, challenging them to confront AIDS positively. I also believe that God has sent me to help the suffering women in Zambia who are hurting because they have the disease or have lost a relative by it. . . .

As I counsel more and more women about AIDS, I have become more interested in the issues of women and AIDS. I would like to highlight some of the issues that women in Zambia are facing today. Women are very vulnerable to HIV infection for several reasons. Traditionally the status of a woman has been lower than that of a man. The man was seen as the hunter and the woman as the conquest. In modern times things have not gotten any better. Women make up the greater percentage of those who cannot read or write in Zambia. As a result, there are relatively very few women in formal salaried employment.

Sources: Positive Women: Voices of Women Living with AIDS, eds. Andrea Rudd and Darien Taylor (Toronto: Second Story Press, 1992), 27–30; www.simplytaty.com.

Within a relationship, it is usually the man who chooses his partner and controls when to have sexual intercourse with her. A woman who is worried about HIV infection or sexually transmitted diseases cannot refuse to have sex with her husband or insist that he use condoms. Accommodation supplied by the government or even by a private company usually belongs to the man. So the need for a home and money to buy essentials for her children and herself often forces the wife to stick to a degrading marriage situation. This unfair situation exists not only in marriage. Young girls are pressured to have sex. There is the sugar daddy, who exploits the innocence and the economic vulnerability of young girls. There is also intense social pressure on single young women to be married. This pushes them into relationships with men whether or not the men are single or married, in order that the women can somehow be counted among those with the status of marriage.

Traditionally, an African woman has her ultimate fulfillment in childbearing. The goal of every woman is to leave behind one or more children of her family or tribe, irrespective of whether she is married or not. If a woman has no children or has only girls, then she will be under considerable pressure to continue childbearing, whether or not she is carrying HIV. Within a marriage, a woman doesn't have much say in issues such as child spacing or family planning, despite the fact that it is her body that is being used for childbearing and childrearing.

Zambia is going through a hard economic period. Women, both married and single, are suffering from the impact of high inflation and lack of formal salaried employment. Many of them are involved in petty trading to raise some money in order to survive. In this situation, the pressure to have sex for money is very high. Because the government does not want to acknowledge that prostitution exists, there is little help when single women demand treatment for sexually transmitted diseases or contraceptives at government clinics. As you can see, the woman in Zambia, the woman in Africa, the woman in the third world, the woman in the world at large is much more vulnerable than a man to HIV infection.

In addition, AIDS is yet another enormous burden to the Zambian woman. Family involvement in the care of the sick at home is common in our culture. At the center of all care is a woman, either as wife, mother, aunt, sister, cousin or even a grandmother. It is the woman who feeds, who washes, clothes and cares of [for] the sick and the dying.

My message to women everywhere is that we must not wait for others to fight our battles for us. I am HIV positive, but AIDS has not beaten me. I will fight this monster and its effects on me personally, on my family and on my community, as long as I am alive. Sisters, reach out to your sisters, and let us remember that when you teach a man, you teach an individual, but that when you teach a woman, you teach and reach a nation.

Nkosi Johnson.   Hi, my name is Nkosi Johnson. I live in Melville, Johannesburg, South Africa. I am 11 years old and I have full-blown AIDS. I was born HIV-positive. When I was two years old, I was living in a care center for HIV/AIDS-infected people. My mommy was obviously also infected and could not afford to keep me because she was very scared that the community she lived in would find out that we were both infected and chase us away. I know she loved me very much and would visit me when she could. And then the care center had to close down because they didn't have any funds. So my foster mother, Gail Johnson, who was a director of the care center and had taken me home for weekends, said at a board meeting she would take me home. She took me home with her and I have been living with her for eight years now. . . .

In 1997 Mommy Gail went to the school, Melpark Primary, and she had to fill in a form for my admission and it said, "Does your child suffer from anything?" so she said yes: AIDS. My Mommy Gail and I have always been open about me having AIDS. And then my Mommy Gail was waiting to hear if I was admitted to school. Then she phoned the school, who said, "We will call you," and then they had a meeting about me. Of the parents and the teachers at the meeting, 50 percent said yes and 50 percent said no. And then on the day of my big brother's wedding, the media found out that there was a problem about me going to school. No one seemed to know what to do with me because I am infected. The AIDS workshops were done at the school for parents and teachers to teach them not to be scared of a child with AIDS. I am very proud to say that there is now a policy for all HIV-infected children to be allowed to go into schools and not be discriminated against. . . .

I hate having AIDS because I get very sick and I get very sad when I think of all the other children and babies that are sick with AIDS. I just wish that the government can start giving AZT to pregnant HIV mothers to help stop the virus being passed on to their babies. Babies are dying very quickly, and I know one little abandoned baby who came to stay with us and his name was Micky. He couldn't breathe, he couldn't eat, and he was so sick, and Mommy Gail had to phone welfare to have him admitted to a hospital, and he died. But he was such a cute little baby, and I think the government must start doing it because I don't want babies to die.

Because I was separated from my mother at an early age, because we were both HIV positive, my Mommy Gail and I have always wanted to start a care center for HIV/AIDS mothers and their children. I am very happy and proud to say that the first Nkosi's Haven was opened last year. And we look after 10 mommies and 15 children. My Mommy Gail and I want to open five Nkosi's Havens by the end of next year because I want more infected mothers to stay together with their children – they mustn't be separated from their children so they can be together and live longer with the love that they need.

When I grow up, I want to lecture to more and more people about AIDS – and if Mommy Gail will let me, around the whole country. I want people to understand about AIDS – to be careful and respect AIDS. You can't get AIDS if you touch, hug, kiss, hold hands with someone who is infected.

Care for us and accept us – we are all human beings. We are normal. We have hands. We have feet. We can walk, we can talk, we have needs just like everyone else. Don't be afraid of us. We are all the same!

NOTES

1. From a study by M. Colvin, "Sexually Transmitted Infections in Southern Africa: A Public Health Crisis," *Southern African Journal of Science* 96 (2000): 335–339, as quoted in Tony Barnett and Alan Whiteside, *AIDS in the Twenty-First Century: Disease and Globalization* (Basingstoke, Hampshire, and New York: Palgrave Macmillian, 2002), 185.
2. *New Vision,* December 3, 1990, as quoted in Maryinez Lyons, "The Point of View: Perspectives on AIDS in Uganda," in *AIDS in Africa and the Caribbean,* eds. George Bond, John Kreniske, Ida Susser, and Joan Vincent (Boulder, CO: Westview Press, 1997), 140.
3. *New Vision,* November 15, 1990 and December 14, 1990, as quoted in Lyons, "Perspectives on AIDS in Uganda," 138–139.
4. Virginia Van der Vliet, "South Africa Divided against AIDS: A Crisis of Leadership," in *AIDS and South Africa: The Social Expression of a Pandemic,* eds. Kyle D. Kauffman and David L. Lindauer (Houndmills, Basingstoke and New York: Palgrave Macmillan, 2004), 58–86; Nicoli Nattrass, *The Moral Economy of AIDS in South Africa* (Cambridge: Cambridge University Press, 2004), 48–55.

Epilogue: Making Connections

It was 1985. As a young journalist in New York City, I was given a new assignment by my editor: to research a terribly frightening disease that had only lately appeared on the scene but already seemed to herald a modern apocalypse. It was, of course, the AIDS epidemic, to which no cure was (or still is) in sight and therefore killed with a pitilessly unfailing mortality. As my colleagues and I prepared a monograph on the toll that the disease was taking on the American workplace, we confronted the human face of the epidemic: co-workers shunned for fear of contracting AIDS from computer keyboards or coffee cups, employees denied health benefits as it became clear that AIDS was a long-term illness, and members of identified "risk groups" discriminated against in both hiring and firing procedures. It was still early in the history of this "plague," when many epidemiological unknowns yet awaited elucidation, and the fear was palpable.

AIDS proved to be a watershed, not only for me personally, but also for many members of my generation, who were in their 20s and 30s during the 1980s and 1990s. This seemed a particularly cruel disease: just as we were entering what should have been a sexually-active period in our lives, the pursuit of such pleasures could now spell our doom. Sex and death were here thrown together in a vividly grotesque embrace. What once was merely a quaint cultural allusion was now quite real. A popular bumper sticker seemed to mark the new spirit of the times: "Remember when sex was safe and Harleys [Harley Davidson motorcycles] were dangerous?" There was the sense that somehow we were being made to pay for the "sins" of our fathers and mothers, who had flaunted their freedoms in the "sexual revolution" of a hopelessly bygone era. A gulf now yawned between us and our envied elders, who, we felt, had never before had to confront so terrifying and intimate challenges to the emotional, moral, and social fabric of their lives. Now nothing could ever be the same. Everything had changed.

Yet despite some alienation from the immediately preceding generation, a strange degree of kinship began to emerge between those of us living – in some form or another – with AIDS and the sufferers of the more distant past who likewise faced over-mighty epidemics. Among the attractions in my now self-assigned duty as an historian is to cover the Black Death of the mid-fourteenth century, a disease episode that presents numerous parallels, as well as contrasts, to our own seismic pandemic of the late twentieth and twenty-first centuries. Could not Petrarch's musings of 1349, "Will posterity believe these things, when we who have seen it can scarcely believe it," not equally well apply to our own times? AIDS is certainly comparable to the Black Death in terms of the sheer mortality and long-lasting effects that it has caused. But it is comparable to other diseases as well, such as syphilis, which likewise has a long incubation period in the victim and is spread by sexual intercourse, or to smallpox, in terms of its debilitating impact upon predominantly poor, developing countries that once had been colonies of the West.

For me, as well as for plenty of other historians, AIDS has posed some new answers, and at the same time reopened old questions. For instance, AIDS has served as a kind of referee of the debate over whether disease should be considered as purely a biological or as a social construct: the positivist/relativist dichotomy alluded to in the introduction of this book. AIDS has clearly demonstrated that a disease can be both: a pathogenic reality with dramatic social and cultural implications. On the one hand, AIDS can be legitimately considered to be a "freak of nature" or an "accident of history": the discovery of the human immunodeficiency virus (HIV) thought to be responsible for AIDS was a spectacular and significant victory in our struggle against the disease. On the other hand, AIDS has certainly been exacerbated and facilitated in its spread by purely human and social factors: the unprecedented access to worldwide and cross-continental travel and trade, the use of hypodermic methods of drug and medicinal injection, the transfusion and preparation of blood products, and the liberalization and collapse of sexual taboos and mores. AIDS has also confirmed some old truths, such as that human societies look for scapegoats – homosexuals, prostitutes, vagabonds – in times of disease crisis, that disease falls hardest on the poor and defenseless, and that different cultures and levels of society react in unique ways to a disease epidemic in their midst. With the failure of modern medicine and science to (so far) find vaccines or cures for AIDS, we seem to be thrown back to a time, going all the way to the Black Death of the Middle Ages, when faith and societal customs were accorded equal weight in combating disease. In a word, AIDS has made all the historical questions asked of past epidemics, from the Black Death to smallpox to modern plague, relevant once again.

As you close this book, think about some of those questions raised by your reading and which will continue to be posed by new diseases, such as AIDS, as well as by some old ones, such as tuberculosis and influenza, that persist into our times. What is the best way to combat a disease? In the absence of a foreseeable cure, should it be through biological or medicinal means alone? Why do some societal groups, such as the poor, continue to be plagued by disease? What can be done to alleviate their susceptibility? Why do almost all members of society fear a coming epidemic? What can be done to prepare for it? Is it conceivable that some would benefit by, even welcome, a disease outbreak? If every epidemic has its economic winners and losers, why is this so and are they always the same? Who, if any, are benefitting economically from the current AIDS pandemic? Who are losing? How does disease interact with other forces or variables moving a society, such as war and civil unrest, trade and travel, and bigotry and discrimination? Trying to find the answers to all these questions is not only a matter of academic or intellectual curiosity, but, in the case of disease, also can be a matter of life or death.

The history of disease will go on, despite once confident predictions of an end to epidemics in our times, and those who now wage the heroic struggle to find elusive cures to our new plagues may find that they have more to learn from the past than had once been thought.

Bibliography

General Works on Disease and History

The touchstone of almost all general studies of disease's role in human history is William H. McNeill, *Plagues and Peoples* (Garden City, NY: Anchor Books/Doubleday, 1976), closely followed by Alfred W. Crosby, *Ecological Imperialism: The Biological Expansion of Europe, 900–1900* (Cambridge: Cambridge University Press, 1986). Before McNeill and Crosby, however, several other authors drew attention to the impact disease could have on historical events, although with considerably less cogency, scope, and persuasiveness: Hans Zinsser, *Rats, Lice and History* (Boston: Little, Brown and Co., 1934); Henry E. Sigerist, *Civilization and Disease* (Chicago: University of Chicago Press, 1943); and Frederick F. Cartwright, *Disease and History* (New York: Thomas Y. Crowell Co., 1972). Some useful reference works include *The Cambridge World History of Human Disease*, ed. Kenneth F. Kiple (Cambridge: Cambridge University Press, 1993); *Plague, Pox and Pestilence*, ed. Kenneth F. Kiple (London: Weidenfeld and Nicolson, 1997); Michael B.A. Oldstone, *Viruses,*

Plagues, and History (Oxford: Oxford University Press, 1998); and Brent Hoff and Carter Smith III, *Mapping Epidemics: A Historical Atlas of Disease* (New York and London: Franklin Watts, 2000). While Sigerist is the leading exponent of the positivist view of disease, the relativist school is represented by Robert P. Hudson, *Disease and Its Control: The Shaping of Modern Thought* (Westport, CT: Greenwood Press, 1983); Claudine Herzlich and Janine Pierret, *Illness and Self in Society,* trans. Elborg Forster (Baltimore: Johns Hopkins University Press, 1987); and Allan M. Brandt, "AIDS and Metaphor: Toward the Social Meaning of Epidemic Disease," in *In Time of Plague: The History and Social Consequences of Lethal Epidemic Disease,* ed. Arien Mack (New York: New York University Press, 1991). Two recent works reevaluate disease history in the light of imperialism and the positivist/relativist debate: Sheldon Watts, *Epidemics and History: Disease, Power and Imperialism* (New Haven: Yale University Press, 1997); and J.N. Hays, *The Burdens of Disease: Epidemics and Human Response in Western History* (New Brunswick, NJ: Rutgers University Press, 1998). One should also consult the collection of thought-provoking essays by Charles E. Rosenberg, *Explaining Epidemics and Other Studies in the History of Medicine* (Cambridge: Cambridge University Press, 1992). The earlier view that disease was a conquerable foe of human progress was advanced in the following: Charles-Edward Amory Winslow, *The Conquest of Epidemic Disease: A Chapter in the History of Ideas* (Princeton, NJ: Princeton University Press, 1943); and L. Fabian Hirst, *The Conquest of Plague: A Study of the Evolution of Epidemiology* (Oxford: Clarendon Press, 1953). Two books that have raised the alarm about the sudden, recent arrival of incurable diseases that cast doubt on human confidence in the end of epidemics include Richard Krause, *The Restless Tide: The Persistent Challenge of the Microbial World* (Washington DC: National Foundation for Infectious Disease, 1981); and Laurie Garrett, *The Coming Plague: Newly Emerging Diseases in a World Out of Balance* (Harmondsworth, Middlesex: Penguin Books, 1994).

The Black Death in Europe and the Middle East

For general studies on the Black Death in Europe during the Middle Ages, see: Philip Ziegler, *The Black Death* (New York: Harper and Row, 1969); Robert S. Gottfried, *The Black Death: Natural and Human Disaster in Medieval Europe* (New York: Free Press, 1983); David Herlihy,

The Black Death and the Transformation of the West, ed. Samuel K. Cohn Jr. (Cambridge, MA: Harvard University Press, 1997); and John Aberth, *From the Brink of the Apocalypse: Confronting Famine, War, Plague, and Death in the Later Middle Ages* (New York: Routledge Press, 2000). Important collections of essays about the Black Death include *The Black Death: A Turning Point in History?* ed. William M. Bowsky (New York: Holt, Rinehart and Winston, 1971); and *The Black Death: The Impact of the Fourteenth-Century Plague*, ed. Daniel Williman (Binghamton, NY: Center for Medieval and Early Renaissance Studies, 1982). Both Graham Twigg, *The Black Death: A Biological Reappraisal* (New York: Schocken Books, 1984) and J.F.D. Shrewsbury, *A History of Bubonic Plague in the British Isles* (Cambridge: Cambridge University Press, 1970) challenge identification of the Black Death with plague on what they claim is the insufficient transmission ability of the rat–flea nexus in the spread of bubonic plague. More recently, Samuel K. Cohn Jr., *The Black Death Transformed: Disease and Culture in Early Renaissance Europe* (London and New York: Arnold and Oxford University Press, 2002) makes this argument in the context of an intensive study of medieval sources, including chronicles, plague tracts, and wills, as well as of the records of the Plague Research Commission that studied modern bubonic plague in India at the turn of the twentieth century. However, Cohn's arguments and interpretations are not universally accepted and are quite controversial, nor does he propose an alternative for plague as the causative disease of the Black Death. Good collections of primary sources on the Black Death include: John Aberth, *The Black Death: The Great Mortality of 1348–1350. A Brief History with Documents* (Boston and New York: Bedford/St. Martin's Press, 2005); and *The Black Death*, ed. Rosemary Horrox (Manchester: Manchester University Press, 1994).

An important study of the Black Death from the Muslim and Middle Eastern perspective is Michael W. Dols, *The Black Death in the Middle East* (Princeton, NJ: Princeton University Press, 1977). For the social and economic impacts of the Black Death, one can start with the classic accounts by John Hatcher, *Plague, Population and the English Economy, 1348–1530* (London: Macmillan, 1977); David Herlihy, "Deaths, Marriages, Births, and the Tuscan Economy (ca.1300–1550)," in *Population Patterns in the Past*, ed. Ronald Demos Lee (New York: Academic Press, 1977); and Jim Bolton, " 'The World Upside Down': Plague as an Agent of Social and Economic Change," in *The Black Death in England*, ed. W.M. Ormrod and Phillip G. Lindley

(Stamford, Lincolnshire: Watkins, 1996). Two works that study the Black Death's effect on women's work in the medieval economy include P.J.P. Goldberg, *Women, Work, and Life Cycle in a Medieval Economy: Women in York and Yorkshire, c. 1300–1520* (Oxford: Oxford University Press, 1992); and Mavis E. Mate, *Daughters, Wives, and Widows after the Black Death: Women in Sussex, 1350–1535* (Woodbridge, Suffolk: Boydell and Brewer, 1998). Good accounts in English of the Flagellant movement and the Jewish pogroms during the Black Death include Richard Kieckhefer, "Radical Tendencies in the Flagellant Movement of the Mid-Fourteenth Century," *Journal of Medieval and Renaissance Studies* 4 (1974): 157–176; and M. Bruer, "The 'Black Death' and Antisemitism," in *Antisemitism through the Ages,* ed. S. Almog and trans. N.H. Reisner (Oxford and New York: Pergamon Press, 1988). To place the Black Death pogroms within the context of medieval attitudes toward the Jews throughout the Middle Ages, one should also consult the following works: Gavin I. Langmuir, *Toward a Definition of Antisemitism* (Berkeley and Los Angeles: University of California Press, 1990); idem, *History, Religion, and Antisemitism* (Berkeley and Los Angeles: University of California Press, 1990); Kenneth R. Stow, *Alienated Minority: The Jews of Medieval Latin Europe* (Cambridge, MA: Harvard University Press, 1992); Stephen T. Katz, *The Holocaust in Historical Context. Volume 1: The Holocaust and Mass Death before the Modern Age* (New York: Oxford University Press, 1994); David Nirenberg, *Communities of Violence: Persecution of Minorities in the Middle Ages* (Princeton, NJ: Princeton University Press, 1996); and Robert Chazan, *Medieval Stereotypes and Modern Antisemitism* (Berkeley and Los Angeles: University of California Press, 1997). For the artistic impact of the Black Death, one should begin with the famous works by Johan Huizinga, *The Waning of the Middle Ages: A Study of the Forms of Life, Thought and Art in France and the Netherlands in the Dawn of the Renaissance,* trans. Frederik Jan Hopman (London: E. Arnold and Co., 1924); and Millard Meiss, *Painting in Florence and Siena after the Black Death: The Arts, Religion, and Society in the Mid-Fourteenth Century* (Princeton, NJ: Princeton University Press, 1951).

Smallpox in the Americas

For general histories of smallpox, see Donald R. Hopkins, *The Greatest Killer: Smallpox in History* (Chicago: University of Chicago Press, 1983); and Jonathan B. Tucker, *Scourge: The Once and Future Threat of*

Smallpox (New York: Atlantic Monthly Press, 2001). An important new work that attempts to synthesize the impact of disease in the new world with the cultural impact of the "Black Legend" in Spanish America is Suzanne Austin Alchon, *A Pest in the Land: New World Epidemics in a Global Perspective* (Albuquerque, NM: University of New Mexico Press, 2003). One should also consult the classic works by Alfred W. Crosby Jr., *The Columbian Exchange: Biological and Cultural Consequences of 1492* (Wesport, CT: Greenwood, 1972); and Noble David Cook, *Born to Die: Disease and New World Conquest, 1492–1650* (Cambridge: Cambridge University Press, 1998). A more geographically focused study that also examines the impact of cultural change in conjunction with disease that was wrought by the Spanish upon indigenous populations is Daniel T. Reff, *Disease, Depopulation, and Culture Change in Northwestern New Spain, 1518–1764* (Salt Lake City, Utah: University of Utah Press, 1991). A useful collection of essays on the topic of disease in the Spanish colonies is *"Secret Judgments of God": Old World Disease in Colonial Spanish America*, eds. Noble David Cook and W. George Lovell (Norman, OK: University of Oklahoma Press, 1992). There are many studies of the population of native America in the context of the Old World disease impact. Some major works include Nicolás Sánchez-Albornoz, *The Population of Latin America: A History*, trans. W.A.R. Richardson (Berkeley and Los Angeles: University of California Press, 1974); Russell Thornton, *American Indian Holocaust and Survival: A Population History* (Norman, OK: University of Oklahoma Press, 1987); Thomas M. Whitmore, *Disease and Death in Early Colonial Mexico: Stimulating Amerindian Depopulation* (Boulder, CO: Westview Press, 1992); *The Native Population of the Americas in 1492*, ed. William M. Denevan, 2nd edn. (Madison, WI: University of Wisconsin Press, 1992); and *Disease and Demography in the Americas*, eds. John W. Verano and Douglas H. Ubelaker (Washington DC: Smithsonian Institution Press, 1992). For works that specifically examine the effect of smallpox, see E. Wagner Stearn and Allen E. Stearn, *The Effect of Smallpox on the Destiny of the Amerindian* (Boston: Bruce Humphries, 1945); John Duffy, "Smallpox and the Indians in the American Colonies," *Bulletin of the History of Medicine* 25 (1951): 324–341; and Francis J. Brooks, "Revising the Conquest of Mexico: Smallpox, Sources, and Populations," *Journal of Interdisciplinary History* 24 (1993): 1–29. Works that specifically focus upon disease among the North American natives include Sherburne F. Cook,

"The Significance of Disease in the Extinction of the New England Indians," *Human Biology* 45 (1973): 485–508; and Douglas H. Ubelaker, "North American Indian Population Size: Changing Perspectives," in *Disease and Demography in the Americas.*

Bubonic and Pneumonic Plague in India and China

India's crisis with bubonic plague at the turn of the twentieth century must be examined within the context of the British government's imperialistic policies toward its colonies. For this perspective, readers should consult the following works: Ira Klein, "Plague, Policy and Popular Unrest in British India," *Modern Asian Studies* 22 (1988): 723–755; I.J. Catanach, "Plague and the Tensions of Empire: India 1896–1918," in *Imperial Medicine and Indigenous Societies*, ed. David Arnold (Manchester: Manchester University Press, 1988); David Arnold, *Colonizing the Body: State Medicine and Epidemic Disease in Nineteenth-Century India* (Berkeley and Los Angeles: University of California Press, 1993); idem, "Touching the Body: Perspectives on the Indian Plague, 1896–1900," in *Selected Subaltern Studies*, eds. Ranajit Guha and Gayatri Chakravorty Spivak (New York: Oxford University Press, 1988); and Mark Harrison, *Public Health in British India: Anglo-Indian Preventive Medicine, 1859–1914* (Cambridge: Cambridge University Press, 1994). The British government also published a voluminous amount of material on its scientific and administrative efforts to combat plague. Among the most important of these publications, at least concerning the early stages of the epidemic, are the Indian Plague Commission's *Minutes of Evidence* and *Report*, published in 5 volumes by Her Majesty's Stationery Office in London between 1900 and 1901. Several published reports by army and Civil Service officers, mainly on the plague in Bombay, are also valuable: W.F. Gatacre, *Report on the Bubonic Plague in Bombay* (Bombay: Times of India Steam Press, 1897); M.E. Couchman, *Account of the Plague Administration in the Bombay Presidency from September 1896 till May 1897* (Bombay, 1897); R. Nathan, *Plague in Northern India, 1896–1897* (Simla, 1898); and J.K. Condon, *The Bombay Plague, being a History of the Progress of Plague in the Bombay Presidency from September 1896 to June 1899* (Bombay: Education Society's Steam Press, 1900). Native newspaper reports on the plague, listed by month and year, are available on microfilm among the India Office Records of the British Library in London. For the pneumonic plague in Manchuria during the first two decades of the twentieth century, one should consult the works by Wu Liande, published under the name of Wu Lien-Teh. The collection of *North Manchurian Plague Prevention Service Reports*, edited by Wu Lien-Teh, was published in three separate volumes: that for 1911–1913 by Cambridge University Press in 1914; that for 1914–1917 by the Peking Gazette Press in 1917; and that for 1918–1922 by the Tientsin Press in 1922. Wu Lien-Teh also published *A Treatise on Pneumonic Plague* (Geneva: Publications of the League of Nations, 1926), and was co-author with J.W.H. Chun, R. Pollitzer, and C.Y. Wu of *Plague: A Manual for Medical and Public Health Workers* (Weishengshu: National Quarantine Service, Shanghai Station, 1936), both of which have large sections devoted to the outbreak of pneumonic plague in Manchuria.

AIDS in sub-Saharan Africa

The most up-to-date statistics on the prevalence of AIDS around the world are available on the UNAIDS website, www.unaids.org. Recent information on the status of AIDS in various countries, including those in sub-Saharan Africa, is also at hand in Tony Barnett and Alan Whiteside, *AIDS in the Twenty-First Century: Disease and Globalization* (Basingstoke, Hampshire, and New York: Palgrave Macmillan, 2002). Comprehensive coverage of the biological and social issues surrounding AIDS in sub-Saharan Africa can be found in several essay compilations: *HIV and AIDS in Africa: Beyond Epidemiology*, eds. Ezekiel Kalipeni, Susan Craddock, Joseph Oppong, and Jayati Ghosh (Oxford: Blackwell Publishing, 2004); *AIDS in Africa*, eds. Max Essex, Souleymane Mboup, Phyllis Kanki, Richard Marlink, and Sheila Tlou, 2nd edn. (New York: Kluwer Academic/Plenum Publishers, 2002); *AIDS in Africa and the Caribbean*, eds. George Bond, John Kreniske, Ida Susser, and Joan Vincent (Boulder, CO: Westview Press, 1997); and *AIDS: An African Perspective*, ed. Al Olufemi Williams (Boca Raton, FL and Ann Arbor, MI: CRC Press, 1992). Works that trace the history and geographical spread of AIDS include Peter Gould, *The Slow Plague: A Geography of the AIDS Pandemic* (Oxford: Blackwell Publishers, 1993); and Gary Shannon, Gerald Pyle, and Rashid Bashshur, *The Geography of AIDS: Origins and Course of an Epidemic* (New York: Guilford Press, 1991). In addition, some works place AIDS within the historical context of other disease pandemics and explore the debate over its cultural definitions: see Mirko D. Grmek, *History of AIDS: Emergence and Origin of a Modern Pandemic*, trans. Russell Maulitz and Jacalyn Duffin (Princeton: Princeton University Press, 1990); and *AIDS: The Burdens of History*, eds. Elizabeth Fee and Daniel M. Fox (Berkeley and Los Angeles: University of California Press, 1988). William A. Rushing's *The AIDS Epidemic: Social Dimensions of an Infectious Disease* (Boulder, CO: Westview Press, 1995) has been attacked for supposedly stereotyping African sexual behaviors as responsible for AIDS' origins and spread; for the opposing point of view, see Richard and Rosalind Chirimutta, *AIDS, Africa, and Racism*, 2nd edn. (London: Free Association Books, 1989). Another polemical work is Alexander Irwin, Joyce Millen, and Dorothy Fallows, *Global AIDS: Myths and Facts: Tools for Fighting the AIDS Pandemic* (Cambridge, MA: South End Press, 2003), which makes the case for AIDS activism, promotes more therapy intervention, and decries scapegoating of AIDS victims. A book on the role that traditional healers in sub-Saharan Africa have played in fighting AIDS and other sexually transmitted diseases is Edward C. Green, *AIDS and STDs in Africa: Bridging the Gap Between Traditional Healing and Modern Medicine* (Boulder, CO: Westview Press, 1994).

A work that focuses on the AIDS epidemic in Uganda is Tony Barnett and Piers Blaikie, *AIDS in Africa: Its Present and Future Impact* (New York: The Guilford Press, 1992). A number of research articles that explore the factors in AIDS' decline in Uganda and the disease's impact upon family households and orphans there are to be found in *The Continuing HIV/AIDS Epidemic in Africa: Responses and Coping Strategies*, eds. I.O. Orubuloye, John C. Caldwell, and James P.M. Ntozi (Canberra: The Australian National University, 1999). This book also contains informative research articles on AIDS in other sub-Saharan African countries, including condom intervention among commercial sex workers, drivers, and students in Nigeria. *AIDS in Africa and the Caribbean* contains, among other essays with a focus on Uganda, the useful article by Maryinez Lyons "The Point of View: Perspectives on AIDS in Uganda," which examines the political context of the response by the Museveni government to AIDS. There is also an essay on the sexual behavior and attitudes toward condom use among Ugandan women in the context of AIDS in *Global AIDS Policy*, ed. Douglas A. Feldman (Westport, CT: Bergin and Garvey, 1994). For good accounts of the denialist response by the Mbeki government of South Africa to the AIDS crisis, and the reactions it has provoked, see Virginia van der Vliet's essay "South Africa Divided against AIDS: A Crisis of Leadership," in *AIDS and South Africa: The*

Social Expression of a Pandemic, eds. Kyle D. Kauffman and David L. Lindauer (Houndmills, Basingstoke and New York: Palgrave Macmillian, 2004); and Nicoli Nattrass, *The Moral Economy of AIDS in South Africa* (Cambridge: Cambridge University Press, 2004). For the early history of South Africa's AIDS crisis under the apartheid regime, see Virginia van der Vliet, "Apartheid and the Politics of AIDS," in *Global AIDS Policy*. Another useful essay on the history of AIDS' progress in South Africa is Kyle D. Kauffman's essay, "Why is South Africa the HIV Capital of the World? An Institutional Analysis of the Spread of a Virus," in *AIDS and South Africa*. A good study of the social and cultural factors behind the spread of AIDS in South Africa is Liz Walker, Graeme Reid, and Morna Cornell, *Waiting to Happen: HIV/AIDS in South Africa–The Bigger Picture* (Boulder, CO: Lynne Rienner Publishers, 2004). Books with a focus on AIDS' impact upon women and children in sub-Saharan Africa include Emma Guest, *Children of AIDS: Africa's Orphan Crisis*, 2nd edn. (London and Pietermaritzburg, SA: Pluto Press and University of Natal Press, 2003); *Impacts and Interventions: The HIV/AIDS Epidemic and the Children of South Africa*, eds. Jeff Gow and Chris Desmond (Pietermaritzburg, SA: University of Natal Press, 2002); Carolyn Baylies, Janet Bujra, et al., *AIDS, Sexuality and Gender in Africa: Collective Strategies and Struggles in Tanzania and Zambia* (London and New York: Routledge Press, 2000); *Women, Children, and HIV/AIDS*, eds. Felissa L. Cohen and Jerry D. Durham (New York: Springer Publishing, 1993); and *Positive Women: Voices of Women Living with AIDS*, eds. Andrea Rudd and Darien Taylor (Toronto: Second Story Press, 1992).

Index